Meet The Ma ume n

With Class 786

Youths of HIC Orlando, Florida, 2006

In the Name of Allah (SWT), the Kind, the Merciful

Meet The Masumeen

With Class 786

Published by
Sun Behind The Cloud Publications Ltd
PO Box 15889, Birmingham, B16 6NZ

This edition first published in paperback 2012

A CIP catalogue record for this book is available from the British Library

ISBN 978-1-908110-04-6

Printed in the United Kingdom by Imprint Digital

www.sunbehindthecloud.com

A Word from the Authors

Inspiration, an eleven letter word with immense power, by definition is a "divine influence directly and immediately exerted upon the mind or soul." The book you hold is a proof of how powerful inspiration can be.

This book originated from a weekly Youth Group discussion with an inspirational speaker, Sister Tahera Kassamali. Her ability to show the Aimmah in a light that we could relate to in our daily lives made us look at them like never before. She lit the flame of inspiration in our hearts and Allah SWT's plan was in motion.

This inspiration was further kindled by a suggestion from another amazing speaker, Sister Masooma Hassan. When asked what is the one thing the youths should focus on that year, she suggested Shia Children's books". She explained the lack of well written books for the children of our communities. She took the candle that was lit with the flame of inspiration from Taherabai and gave it a beautiful holder, and inspired us even further.

The HIC Youths were thus inspired to write a kids' book on the 14 Masumeen. This project was truly a team effort. The hard work of the researchers, authors, illustrators, and editors kept the light of inspiration from flickering even at the face of financial and time constraints. Allah SWT guided us and helped us through with this project.

We have tried our best to ensure that all the stories about the Masumeen are based on authentic traditions and popular literature and the text has been checked by scholars. As the goal of this book is to inspire children by the moral traits of the Masumeen, the details of some of stories have been simplified. The charaters and the fantasy of time-travel are of course fictional!

We thank Allah for this opportunity for helping our project materialize by blessing us with a wonderful team of authors, illustrators, editors, and publisher. We hope and pray the book can light the flame of inspiration in the hearts of our readers to follow the footsteps of the Masumeen. We pray the Almighty accepts what little we have done and that He reward us by letting us answer the Awaited one's call.

Labayk Ya Imam!

Story Boards by the Youths of HIC
Aliya Alidina
Binte Abbas
Rumina Hassan
Tasnim Jagani
Sameer Jagani
Sajida Jivraj
Sabiha Kassam
Shazia Yusufali
Zahra Sachoo
Kaniz-e-Zahrah

Story Boards Transformations
Binte Abbas, Ibn Ali, and Kaniz-e-Zahrah

Illustration Team
Rumina Hassan and Shazia Yusufali

Editing Team
Masooma Hassan, Shaheen Merali, Musarrat Dewji, Rumina Hassan, and Kaniz-e-Zahrah

Contents

Faith
Prophet Muhammed
(SAW)

It was a beautiful, bright sunny day. The pleasant sounds of birds chirping and soaring through the air were overshadowed by car doors being slammed, and children saying "Fi-Amanillah" to parents. Children of all ages were rushing up the stairs trying to avoid being late. The hustle and bustle of trying to make it into the classroom before the tardy bell was in the air. This was the normal routine for many of the students at Al-Iman Madrassah.

Walking through the crowded hallway was Mr. Hashim, the Principle of the school. With him, was a kind, gentle woman named Mrs. Hudda. She seemed very polite while he was babbling away. He suddenly stopped in front of Class 786, and with a sweaty, tensed, palm grabbed the rusty, silver knob.

He took a deep breath as he opened the door...

No one inside the classroom could hear the squeaking door as it opened. As usual, Class 786 was a mess!

The desks and chairs were upside down. The students were chatting away, some were yelling; others were fighting. There was paper everywhere! Some of the boys were having a paper ball fight while others made paper 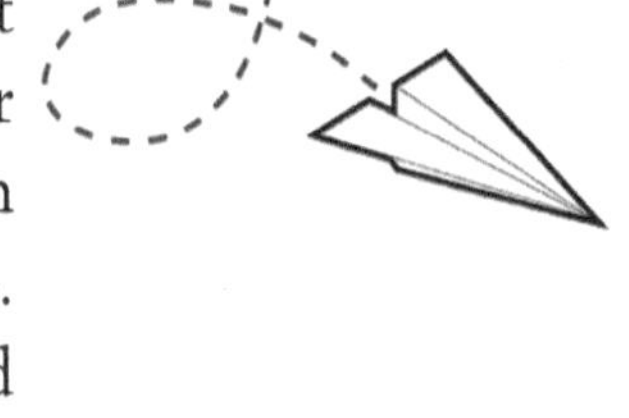 airplanes and threw them across the classroom. Mrs. Hudda remained composed and ducked to avoid being hit. Mr. Hashim tried  to calm them down but nobody paid any attention to him. They just continued with their racket. He glanced at Mrs. Hudda who didn't even flinch with all the craziness going on. She had a smile on her face and the aura of patience and peace in her attitude.

"Mrs. Hudda, they are all yours! Hope you can handle this crowd. After all, you are our last option and we have very high hopes in you. You come with great references. Maybe you can work your magic on these mischief-makers!" Mr. Hashim said expectantly.

"Mr. Hashim, have hope only in Allah SWT and nobody else. What I can do here is only with the help of the Almighty. InshAllah we will turn these children around into good, faithful and pious Muslims. However, before I agree to teach this class, I need you to promise me one thing. I would like to take this class on a field trip at the end of the semester as part of this Islamic History class," Mrs. Hudda asked confidently.

Mr. Hashim looked around the chaotic room and with a smirk replied, "You want to take THIS class on a field trip? Sure, if you can handle them! I leave you under Allah SWT's mercy. Good luck! You will definitely need it!" As he quickly walked away he murmured under his breath, "I bet she won't even last for two weeks."

Mrs. Hudda looked around and saw the kids yelling and screaming in every nook and cranny of the classroom. From the corner of her eyes she saw a boy sitting on a chair in tattered and torn clothes nearly in tears, and a group of boys standing around him and teasing him. "Sibtain never has a bath," they sneered.

The ring leader was a tall, light-haired boy named Yasir. Mrs. Hudda watched as Sibtain stood up and kicked Yasir on his knees. "It serves you right for teasing me like that!" yelled Sibtain.

With his eyes welling up, Yasir shouted back, "You didn't have to kick me for that!" The two boys started fighting. The others started circling around them, cheering for their favorite classmate.

Mrs. Hudda turned to the other side of the class. She saw the girls chatting away, totally oblivious to what was going on in the other side of the classroom. Sitting at her desk, hoarding her belongings, Sabira snapped, "That's mine! I'm not going to share it with you!" Asiya, sounding insulted, replied "FINE! BE LIKE THAT! I'm not going to share my special book that my mom bought from Cairo with you either."

Mrs. Hudda took a deep breath, said 'Bismillah' and recited verses 25-28 from Surah Taha:

قَالَ رَبِّ اشْرَحْ لِي صَدْرِي

He said: O my Lord! Expand my breast for me,

وَيَسِّرْ لِي أَمْرِي

And make my affair easy to me,

وَاحْلُلْ عُقْدَةً مِنْ لِسَانِي

And loose the knot from my tongue,

يَفْقَهُوا قَوْلِي

(That) they may understand my word;

13

She walked to the front of the classroom. She noticed a rundown library section with cobwebs around the shelves and dust all over the place. It looked abandoned, as if nobody had touched the books in years.

She quickly pulled out a thick green book. As she opened it, a beautiful light came out from the book. The light was so bright and illuminating that it captured the attention of the whole class. Everyone stopped doing what they were doing and looked around with amazement; some looking at the book and some looking at the stranger holding the book.

Shabbir and Fizza, puzzled, blurted out, "Who is that lady?" "What's that light?" Hadi rolled his eyes and answered Shabbir, "Yo bro! That's our new teacher. Didn't you see her come in with the Principal? Man you LOVE sleeping!"

Sumayya pushed through the two boys laughing at each other and wondered what book Mrs. Hudda had in her hands. Several of the other children were also curious and timidly walked towards the teacher. As they approached her, they saw her sit down on the wooden, worn out rocking chair and heard her reading in Arabic from the book.

شَهِدَ اللَّهُ أَنَّهُ لَا إِلَهَ إِلَّا هُوَ وَالْمَلَائِكَةُ وَأُولُو الْعِلْمِ قَائِمًا بِالْقِسْطِ ۚ لَا إِلَهَ إِلَّا هُوَ الْعَزِيزُ الْحَكِيمُ

The Arabic words softly rolled out of her mouth and seemed to have a calming effect on the kids - as if it struck the core of their hearts. Hadi was mesmerized and uttered, "Wow!! What does that mean? Man, it sounds so much like what my Grandma keeps reciting."

Mrs. Hudda replied with a grin, "These are verses from the Holy Qur'an, the book Allah SWT has sent as a guide for us. This particular verse is from the chapter of Aale Imran verse 18 where Allah SWT says:

"Allah bears witness Himself that there is no God except Him. And so do the Angels, and all those who have knowledge; keeping His creation in justice, they say there is no God except Him, the Almighty and the Most Wise."

"That's deep dude!" Jawaad exclaimed. Mrs. Hudda laughed and continued, "This verse is a very inspirational one because Allah SWT Himself witnesses His oneness with the angels and those who have knowledge. The verse also shows the significance of gaining knowledge. That's the reason we are all here, because we don't want to be blind believers, we want to believe and understand what we believe in."

Aliya turned to Sayyada and whispered, "I think I really like Mrs...." and then turned to the teacher "Umm...what's your name, Auntie?" "I'm Mrs. Hudda, I'll be your new fifth grade History teacher," came the reply. "I hope we can learn more about Islam from each other so that each one of us can be successful in the eyes of Allah SWT."

Prompted by Mrs. Hudda, the children started introducing themselves one by one and seemed very excited to have a new teacher as cool as Mrs. Hudda. After everyone got to know each other a little better, Mrs. Hudda told the class that since today was the first day of the class, it was the perfect time to teach the kids about the Holy Prophet of Islam, Prophet Muhammed (SAW). It was the Holy Prophet (SAW) that introduced Islam to humanity.

The children saw that she had a little twinkle in her eye. She told them that she had a little surprise for them. Mrs. Hudda asked them to gather around and place their right hand on the Holy Qu'ran and repeat after her "LABAYK YA IMAM."

All the kids rushed up to her and put their right hands on the Holy Qu'ran and said, "LABAYK YA…." Before they even finished, a triangular piece made of clay fell out of the Qur'an and Sibtain picked it up. He looked at the piece of clay and read out loud the word engraved on it: "FAITH". He looked at Mrs. Hudda confused.

"Don't worry… it will all make sense eventually," she replied. "Let's go see what the Holy Prophet Muhammed (SAW) has to teach us about faith and knowledge."

Looking at all the kids' hands on the Qu'ran, she asked them to say the special words again.

"Here I am O my Imam" the children yelled.

In the blink of an eye, a beautiful ray of light surrounded the children and they were zapped to a place they had never seen before.

They slowly opened their eyes and were blinded by the bright, shining sun. The children were a bit scared; they didn't know where they were. It was a strange land. There were no tall buildings or cars in sight. No beauty salons or stores like they knew, nothing but old style basic buildings, camels and sand everywhere.

"Where are we?" asked Asiya. Mrs. Hudda saw the children's eyes widen as she explained to them that they had travelled to the past - to the time of the Holy Prophet (SAW). It was a time when Islam was introduced to the world as the final religion from Allah SWT. 

The children were thrilled! They couldn't believe how awesome Mrs. Hudda was and how great it was to be in Mecca! She told them to quickly follow her and they did. The children quietly filtered into a dimly lit room with a long table, surrounded by chairs. They saw a tall, handsome Arab man in a white kandura robe, with a glowing face. He looked so humble, so pious, as if he had

Allah SWT's blessings showering all over him. His presence seemed to bring peace in the hearts of the children. Standing next to the Arab man was a young boy who resembled him very much. The two were making arrangements at the table. It seemed like they were expecting guests for a special meal for a special occasion.

Not too long after, the men of this Arab man's family started coming into the room where Mrs. Hudda and her class were. The Arab man stood at the door welcoming his guests, and urging them to take a seat. All the members of the family arrived and began to eat, and the young boy ensured that everything was in order. When the meal was finished, the Arab man stood and told all his guests why he had invited them. He started to explain. He told them that he had received a revelation from Allah SWT and a command to declare Allah's oneness and his Prophethood to his relatives and kinsmen.

The people in the room stared at him – some with their eyes wide open and others with a mean smirk on their face. The man continued to explain that there is no God but Allah SWT and that he had been appointed as the final Messenger of Allah.

He then asked his kinsmen, "From amongst you, who will be my helper, aid, and successor in my mission?" Nobody responded except the young boy who had been helping him with the arrangements.

The young boy exclaimed

The students from Class 786 started smiling as they got a warm tingling sensation. They just realized who the man was. It was none other than the Holy Prophet Muhammed (SAW) and the young boy was Imam Ali (AS), the cousin of the Prophet (SAW) and his chosen successor.

Some of the men started making fun of the Holy Prophet (SAW), saying that he had lost his mind and was crazy. They told him that he did not know what he was talking about. In mockery, some asked him whatever made him think that they would leave their more than 300 idols for his one Allah. Others mocked the young boy and his father, Abu Talib, who were silently seated in the chairs.

The Holy Prophet (SAW) tried to explain to the men and convince them that their gods were helpless and couldn't even defend themselves if the need arose. How could they ever benefit anybody else? He tried to explain to them the Oneness of Allah, Allah's power, and Allah's might. Some of the men were so arrogant that they continued to mock him and then some of them walked out of the room. The Holy Prophet (SAW) did not give up. The children could see the faith, the sincerity on his glorious face. He knew he was on the right path and nothing the people said or did would make him stop doing what Allah SWT had commanded him to do.

The children discussed what they had just seen and started walking out of the room. Mrs. Hudda instructed them to gather around the Holy Qur'an again and put their hands on it. This time they arrived to a time a few days after the dinner they had just witnessed. They found themselves in the streets, at a time when the Holy Prophet (SAW) had started preaching to the rest of the Meccans. They saw the various reactions the Meccans had to the new message. A handful of them accepted the message of the Holy Prophet (SAW) and considered him as the savior for mankind from the ignorance that was so common at the time.

However, many mocked the Holy Prophet (SAW), threw stones at him and did everything they could think of to get him to give up his divine task.

The children had always heard the stories of the difficult time the Holy Prophet Muhammed (SAW) had in preaching Islam, but they had never imagined how much hardship he had to endure. Seeing the Prophet (SAW) being mocked and hit with stones brought tears to the eyes of the children.

The children followed the Holy Prophet Muhammed (SAW) as he walked towards the mosque. From a window of a building he was passing by, they saw an old lady dump a trash can full of garbage on him.

Prophet Muhammed (SAW) did not get angry at all. Instead he quietly cleaned himself up and continued walking towards the mosque. Sibtain couldn't hold it in anymore, the excitement was killing him, "WAIT A MINUTE! That's the story of the Holy Prophet (SAW) and the old lady, OH MY GOD! Did you see how calm he was? Oh, I would just be ready to beat her up!"

Sayyada, having not heard the story before, asked, "What old lady?"

Ammar proudly started to explain, "Every time the Prophet Muhammed (SAW) went to the mosque, there was an old lady who would dump trash on him. She would do this to him every single time, and just like we saw today, he would never get mad at her."

Before the children could ask more questions, Mrs. Hudda told them to quickly follow the Holy Prophet Muhammed (SAW). They followed Prophet Muhammed (SAW) to the mosque. At the mosque, they saw some people worshipping and another group sitting in a circle discussing. The Holy Prophet Muhammed (SAW) walked toward the group that was deep in discussion and he joined them.

The whole class was astonished at the Holy Prophet (SAW)'s choice. Mrs. Hudda explained that Prophet Muhammed (SAW) valued education just as much as worship. She went on to explain that there should be a balance. Not only should you worship Allah SWT, but you should also think and discuss religion with others so that you learn more. Mrs. Hudda continued to explain that the Holy Prophet (SAW) would sit with his companions in a circle where everyone contributed, asked questions and learned from each other. This was called a 'halaqa'.

As the class watched the halaqa, they noticed a poor man entering the mosque in his torn clothes. The poor man went and sat next to a wealthy, well-dressed man. The rich man was disturbed and tried to pull the edges of his cloak towards himself so the poor man did not touch them.

The Holy Prophet Muhammed (SAW) saw this and was very hurt to see his follower acting like that. The Prophet (SAW) asked the rich man: "Perhaps you are afraid that his poverty will affect you?"

The rich man, ashamed, responded: "No, O Messenger of Allah."

The Prophet (SAW) said: "Then perhaps you are frightened about some of your wealth flying away to him?"

The rich man, overcome with humiliation, replied: "No, O Messenger of Allah."

The Prophet (SAW) then asked him: "Or, you feared that your clothes would become dirty if he touched them?"

The rich man responded: "No, O Messenger of Allah."

The Prophet (SAW) then asked him: "Then why did you draw yourself and your clothes away from him?"

The rich man replied: "I admit that was the most undesirable thing to do. It was an error and I confess my guilt. Now to make amends for it I will give away half of my wealth to this Muslim brother so that I may be forgiven."

The Holy Prophet (SAW) turned to the poor man and asked him, "Do you accept this brother's offer?"

The poor man answered: "I forgive him, but I do not want the wealth that will make me proud like him."

The children couldn't believe their eyes. Seeing the sparks in their eyes, Mrs. Hudda started to explain further. "You see kids, the Holy Prophet (SAW) did not like it when one man tried to humiliate a fellow Muslim. It doesn't matter if you are rich, poor or have some disability. We are all the same in the eyes of Allah SWT because we are all created by Him."

After the discussion was over, the Holy Prophet (SAW) stood up and headed home. Mrs. Hudda and the kids followed him. As they passed by the building that the old lady lived in, they noticed the Prophet (SAW) looking up as if he was looking for someone. He walked to a man standing underneath a balcony and asked him where the old lady who lived above was. The man informed him that she had become ill. Once again, the Holy Prophet (SAW) looked up at the balcony and instead of going home, he walked up the stairs. He knocked on the door. All the students hurried to follow him. They were curious to see what Prophet Muhammed (SAW) intended to do.

"Yup! This is the perfect time for Prophet Muhammed (SAW) to teach the old lady a lesson for being so mean to him and hurting him," Sibtain snickered. The maid opened the door and let Prophet Muhammed (SAW) inside. He walked over to where the old lady was laying. The Prophet (SAW) greeted the old lady. The old lady responded fearfully, "I know why you have come here. You have come to take revenge for the trash that I used to throw on you."

Prophet Muhammed (SAW) smiled at the old lady and answered gently, "Dear lady, I have not come here to take revenge or yell at you. I have come to visit you because you are ill. I pray for you to get better."

The kids could not believe what they had heard. This was the same lady that used to throw garbage at the Holy Prophet (SAW). Here he was being nice to her when she had been so mean to him! The old lady immediately realized her mistake. She could see through his actions how pure and sincere the Holy Prophet Muhammed (SAW) was, and she asked him for forgiveness. Then at that point, she decided to convert to Islam. The Holy Prophet (SAW) helped her recite the Shahada - the verses of the Kalimah that should be recited when you become a Muslim.

The students were all shocked! Mrs. Hudda looked at them and reminded them, "It is not a big deal if you are nice to people who are nice to you, BUT it is a big deal when you are nice to people who are mean to you and hurt you. Remember how you act with those around you is what makes a difference. Our actions have to match our faith." After hearing this, Sibtain and Yasir's eyes met in shame as they remembered how they acted in the classroom with each other. "Okay, we better get going because our class time will almost be over. Now put your hands on the Holy Qur'an and repeat after me, 'LAYBBAK YA IMAM.'"

Just as the children uttered those words, they were all zapped back into the classroom. As they arrived back in the classroom, they could not believe what they had just experienced. Were they dreaming or did they really go back in time and see the Holy Prophet Muhammed (SAW)? Before they could say anything, Mrs. Hudda told them all to sit down in a circle to start their own classroom halaqa. Mrs. Hudda wrote down some facts about the Holy Prophet (SAW) on the chalkboard. The children eagerly wrote them down in their notebooks.

Name: Prophet Muhammed Mustafa (SAW)

Titles: Sadiq (The Truthful), Ameen (The Trustworthy)

Father's Name: Abdullah

Mother's Name: Aamina

Birthday: 17 Rabbi Awal, The year of the elephant

Born: in Mecca

Beloved Wife: Lady Khadijah (AS)

Children: Lady Fatema (AS)

Died on: 28 Safar 11 Hijri at the age of 63 and buried in Medina

Mrs. Hudda then went around the circle and asked each child to share something they saw in their trip that had inspired them.

Sayyada: "I learned that education is very important in Islam."

Sabira: "We need to be nice to each other and share our belongings."

Yasir: "Islam does not like pride so I definitely need to apologize to Sibtain for teasing him."

Sibtain: "Hey, that's cool, because I shouldn't have kicked you either. I learned something too. It's very important to control your anger and be good to others even though they are bad to you. If you have faith in Allah SWT, your actions have to match it."

Sibtain pulled out the triangular piece that he had picked up before they travelled to the past. "The Holy Prophet had faith in Allah SWT. Even though he faced many challenges in spreading the true religion, he never lost faith in Allah SWT. It was his faith that helped him to be successful in everything he did." Sibtain looked at the shiny triangular clay piece that said 'Faith' and placed it around his neck to always remind him to have faith like the Holy Prophet (SAW).

Mrs. Hudda looked at the wall clock and noticed that class was almost over. "Well done children! I think today we have definitely learned some awesome stuff. I really enjoyed being your teacher and I have a feeling that we are going to have some great adventures over the next 13 weeks! I just can't wait to see where we will go next!"

 DING DING DING!! 

As the bells rang, all the children ran up to her and gave her a warm hug. Sibtain whispered to Mrs. Hudda, "Thank you Mrs. Hudda. You are just what our class needs - someone who has faith in us. I am so glad you are our teacher!"

Mrs. Hudda gently hugged all the children as they started to leave the classroom. "See you all next week, inshAllah!" With a twinkle in her eye, she looked around the quiet room, walked towards the worn-out, wooden rocking chair and opened the Holy Qur'an.

Use this page to jot down anything you learned and that you think you can apply to your life.

Salaat
Imam Ali (A.S)

For the first time, the students of Class 786 ran up the stairs of Al-Iman Madrassah excited to be there. They zoomed through all the chaos in the hallway and stopped at the door of Class 786, took a deep breath, and quietly entered the room.

They noticed Mrs. Hudda already seated in the rocking chair, surrounded by a shining light, with her back facing them. They could hear her reciting the Holy Qur'an. Quietly, they tip-toed towards her and sat down on the halaqa rug. Mrs. Hudda smiled at the eager children when she noticed them.

Talib asked, "What were you reciting, Mrs. Hudda?"

Mrs. Hudda responded, "I was reciting verse 55 from Surah Maidah which says:

إِنَّمَا وَلِيُّكُمُ اللّهُ وَرَسُولُهُ

Verily your Guardian is only Allah and His messenger,

وَالَّذِينَ آمَنُوا

and those who believe,

الَّذِينَ يُقِيمُونَ الصَّلَاةَ

those who establish prayers,

وَيُؤْتُونَ الزَّكَاةَ وَهُمْ رَاكِعُونَ

and pay the zakaat while bowing.

Talib looking puzzled questioned, "How can you give charity while bowing? Doesn't that mean giving zakaat in rukuh?"

Mrs. Hudda's face lit up instantly and with a twinkle in her eyes she said, "I am sure Imam Ali (AS) can show us how!" The children smiled as they watched her walk over to the bookshelf and take out a red book.

She then explained, "This is Nahjul Balagha, a collection of sermons and sayings of Imam Ali (AS)."

As she opened the book, a light captured the room once again. The kids gathered around her and put their hands on the book and repeated the blessed words after her:

"LABAYK YA IMAM"

Just like the last time, before the children finished, another small triangular clay piece fell out of the book. This time it had 'Salaat' engraved on it. Yasir picked it up and put it in his pocket. The kids all together again said, "LABAYK YA IMAM" "Here I am O my Imam" and they were zapped to the holy land of Mecca.

The children found themselves in front of the Holy Kaaba. However, it looked very different from the pictures they had seen. It was a simple square building made of brick. The people around it did not even look like Muslims. There were also statues surrounding the Kaaba! Mrs. Hudda explained that they were in Mecca at a time when Prophet Muhammed (SAW) had not yet declared his Prophethood, and most of the Meccans were idol worshippers.

The students noticed a pregnant woman slowly walking towards the Kaaba. She looked like she was in a lot of pain. Mrs. Hudda told them that this was Fatema bint Asad, the mother of Imam Ali (AS).

The children's jaws dropped when they saw the wall of the Kaaba suddenly crack open as she went towards it. As she walked into the Kaaba, the wall closed up behind her. Mrs. Hudda told the children that Fatema bint Asad stayed in the Kaaba for three days. Placing their hands on the red book, the children and Mrs. Hudda then travelled three days forward.

The class found themselves at the same place. They saw Fatema bint Asad come out of the Kaaba holding a radiant baby in her hands. Her worried relatives surrounded her, but the baby did not open his eyes. The Holy Prophet Muhammed (SAW) came and held the baby in his arms. The baby then opened his eyes and the first person he saw was the Holy Prophet (SAW).

Sayyada started to cry, "This baby is Imam Ali (AS), the successor of the Prophet!"

Ammar turned towards her puzzled and said, "Why are you crying? We are supposed to be happy!" Sayyada sniffled, "These are tears of joy, silly!" she snapped back. "Imam Ali (AS) is the first and only person to be born in the Kaaba. I feel honored to be a Shia – his follower." Ammar smiled back, "Good to know you are okay."

Mrs. Hudda overheard the kids talking about what they had just seen and asked them to gather around her. The children formed a circle and talked about the birth of Imam Ali (AS). As they were talking, the sky got darker and darker. All of sudden, the children realized they were no longer by the Kaaba. Sumayya screamed as she and the other children noticed 40 men standing in a circle with their swords, ready to attack.

Mrs. Hudda told the children that they were outside the house of the Holy Prophet (SAW) and it was the night of hijrah, when the Holy Prophet migrated from Mecca to Medina. The men outside his house were from the tribe of Quraysh, who hated the Prophet (SAW) and had come on a mission to kill him. The kids peeked through a cracked window and saw the Holy Prophet talking to Imam Ali.

Mrs. Hudda told the children that by this time, Prophet Muhammed (SAW) had proclaimed his Prophethood and Imam Ali (AS) had been one of the first to accept the true message that the Prophet (SAW) had come with.

The Prophet said to Imam Ali (AS), "Allah SWT has informed me through Angel Jibrail that the unbelievers will break into this house to kill me. I ask you to sleep in my bed.

Imam Ali (AS) asked him, "Will your life be saved by me sleeping in your bed?"

The Prophet (SAW) responded, "Yes."

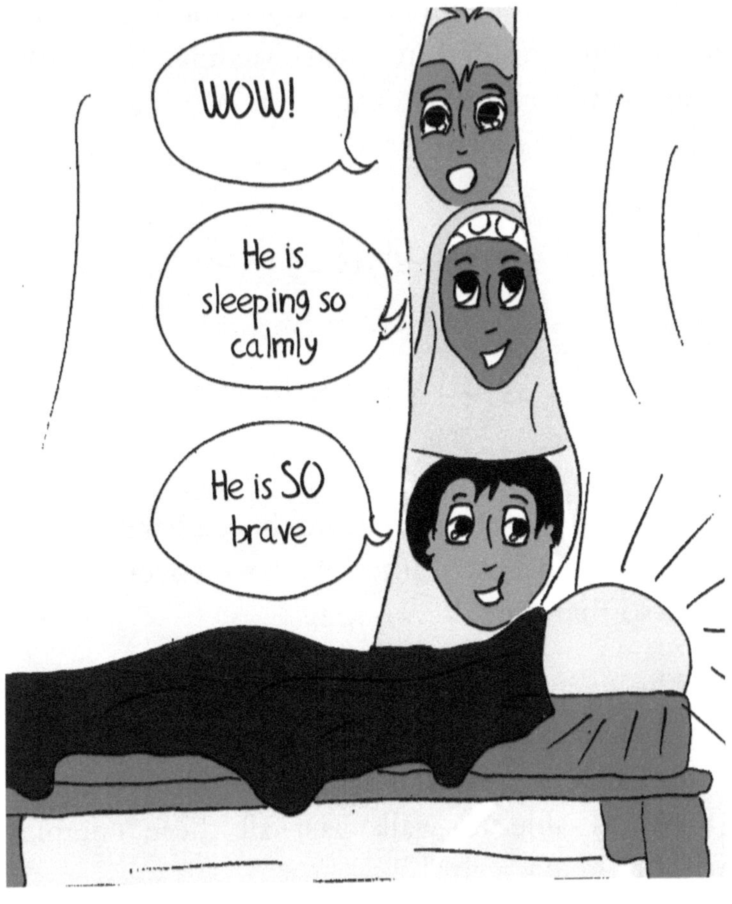

Imam Ali (AS) smiled and accepted to sleep on the bed of the Prophet (SAW), knowing that the life of the Prophet (SAW) would be saved if he did so. Then the time came when the darkness of the night covered everything. Imam Ali (AS) was sleeping on Prophet Muhammed (SAW)'s bed, calmly and peacefully.

Prophet Muhammed (SAW) came out of his house and headed towards Medina. While he walked, the children heard him reciting verse 9 from Surah Yaseen.

وَجَعَلْنَا مِنْ بَيْنِ أَيْدِيهِمْ سَدًّا وَمِنْ خَلْفِهِمْ سَدًّا فَأَغْشَيْنَاهُمْ فَهُمْ لَا يُبْصِرُونَ

"And We have made before them a barrier and a barrier behind them, then We have covered them over so that they do not see..."

The enemies did not even notice him. Fizza, on behalf of all the students, uttered with astonishment, "How is it that the Holy Prophet (SAW) is able to walk past all these enemies without being seen?"

Mrs. Hudda explained that it was the will of Allah SWT and a miracle, protecting the Holy Prophet Muhammed (SAW) from his enemies.

As the night transformed into day, the enemies prepared to attack and barge into the house, ready to kill the Prophet (SAW). The enemies lifted the blanket, ready to strike, only to find Imam Ali (AS) lying on the bed of the Holy Prophet (SAW).

They immediately moved out of the house and sent a few horsemen to search for the Holy Prophet (SAW). But not very long after, they too returned, defeated and hopeless.

Mrs. Hudda explained to the children that Imam Ali (AS)'s faith was so strong that he trusted Allah SWT and the Prophet (SAW) with his life. In fact, Imam Ali (AS) later used to say that the best sleep he had ever had was on the night of hijrah in the bed of the Prophet (SAW). She continued to tell them that Allah SWT loved this action of Imam Ali (AS) so much that He then revealed this verse of the Holy Qur'an in Surah Baqarah, Verse 207:

"And among men is he who sells his Nafs(self) in exchange for the pleasure of Allah..."

The children gathered around Mrs. Hudda as she took out her pocket size Qur'an and they discussed the verse from Surah Baqarah. When they lifted their heads up, they realized that they were no longer outside the house of the Holy Prophet (SAW). Rather, they were at the doorstep of a masjid where Imam Ali (AS) was praying. Just then, a beggar walked into the masjid.

The beggar called out, "Is there anyone who can help me?" but nobody responded. The beggar called out for help three times. When he did not get a response the last time, he raised his hands and prayed to Allah SWT, "I have come to your house for help and I am returning to the streets empty handed."

Just then the children saw Imam Ali (AS) extended his hand while he was in rukuh and the beggar took the ring from the Imam's finger. The beggar thanked Allah SWT and walked out of the masjid.

"That's what the verse from Surah Maidah was talking about! Yes, I solved the puzzle. I am soooo smart!" Shabbir started boasting. Sabira rolled her eyes and gently reminded Shabbir about being humble.

Before anyone could say anything else, Mrs. Hudda explained, "Imam Ali (AS) was so engrossed in his prayer that he did not hear the beggar calling for help at first. However, Imam Ali (AS) heard the beggar when he complained to Allah SWT because Imam Ali (AS)'s soul was so close to Allah SWT during his prayers. This is why the verse talked about giving the charity while bowing. When the beggar prayed to Allah, Imam Ali (AS) received a command from Allah SWT to let him know that there was a beggar at the doorstep of the masjid."

With a sense of satisfaction, the children put their hands on the Nahjul Balagha and repeated after Mrs. Hudda, "LABAYK YA IMAM," and with a flash they were all zapped back to the classroom. They sat down in a circle to form their halaqa and started discussing what they had seen and learnt from Imam Ali (AS).

The children were mesmerized as to how close Imam Ali (AS) was to Allah SWT during his prayers. His soul heard the cries of the beggar not on earth but in the  heavens when the beggar prayed to Allah SWT. How amazing was it that on hearing the call of the beggar, Allah SWT commanded Imam Ali (AS) to extend his hand and give his ring as zakaat to the beggar?

Mrs. Hudda, hearing the children's admiration, told them that Imam Ali (AS) was very devoted to Allah SWT from the moment he was born in the Kaaba, to the time he took his last breath after being wounded in sajdah in Masjid Kufa. Just then, something in Yasir's pocket started glowing. Yasir pulled out the triangular piece that had the word 'Salaat' written on it.

Before Yasir could say anything, Jawaad interrupted, "Mrs. Hudda, my daddy told me a story about Imam Ali (AS) before I went to bed last night. Can I share it with the class?" "Oh please Mrs. Hudda," pleaded Asiya, "Jawaad's dad is a great story-teller." Mrs. Hudda nodded in approval and Jawaad began his story. "One day, Imam Ali (AS) was wounded in battle by an arrow that had struck him on his foot. It was very painful and no one could remove it without hurting the Imam. The Holy Prophet (SAW) suggested to the people that the best time to remove it would be while Imam Ali (AS) was praying. The companions did what the Prophet (SAW) suggested and Imam Ali (AS) did not even flinch because he was so devoted to Allah SWT and so dedicated in his prayer that he didn't feel the pain of the arrow being taken out." "Whoa!" exclaimed Hadi. "How come we can't ever concentrate like that?!"

Aliya nodded in agreement and said, "The moment I start to pray, I remember where I put my toys that I was looking for or what I want to eat for lunch."

Yasir shouted out, "Yeah, me too! I think about my DS, iTouch, and my mom's chicken samosas!"

Mrs. Hudda told the children that they have to build a special relationship with Allah SWT. They need to love Him and be very close to Him. This closeness will help them concentrate in their prayers. She explained to them that if our prayers are not accepted, none of our other good deeds are accepted either. Praying is our way of talking to Allah SWT.

"You know Mrs. Hudda, my dad told me, that when we go pray, we should wear clean and nice clothing. Not just wear normal clothes, because we are going in front of our Lord. He also said that, we should put some perfume. Maybe if we do that, it will also help us concentrate in our salaat, because we are getting physically and mentally ready. Telling our soul, the outside is clean and ready to pray, now you get ready to connect with our Lord spiritually," Imran shared with eagerness.

"That makes so much sense! If I had to meet anyone special, I wouldn't go in my pyjamas, I would take the time to get ready. When I pray, I am preparing for MY Lord and HE is the most important! Thanks Bro - that rocks! This might help me concentrate more" Yasir was thrilled.

"MashAllah I love the way you guys are thinking.

InshAllah together we will be able to help each other become better Muslims. Now let's go over some basic facts about the life of Imam Ali (AS)," Mrs. Hudda said softly. The children took out their note pads and wrote down the information while discussing the life of Imam Ali (AS) with their classmates.

Imam Ali (as) is amazing because he has so much faith and loves Allah (SWT) so much that when he prays he only thinks about Allah (SWT) and concentrates really hard.

I am going to try my best to only think about Allah (SWT) when I pray... and not chicken samosas

Name: Ali

Mother: Lady Fatema bint Asad

Father: Abu Talib

Title: Ameerul Momineen
        (Leader of the Believers)

Birth: 13 Rajab, 600 A.D.

Birthplace: In the Kaaba

Martyrdom: Struck by Ibn
        Muljim on the 19th of
        Ramadhan, died on 21st
        Ramadhan, 40 A.H.

Buried: in Najaf, Iraq

Places Imam lived: Mecca,
                            Medina, Kufa

Legacy : Sermons and Sayings
compiled into the Nahjul Balagha

The children heard the call to prayers. They all rushed out to do wudhu and join the Madrassah Jama'at prayers. Mr. Hashim watched in astonishment. Class 786 was never on time for Jama'at prayers. Yet today they were all in the first two rows, prepared and ready. Their behavior was outstanding and incredible!

After Jama'at prayers were over, Yasir tied the triangular piece saying 'Salaat' around his neck and whispered to Ammar, "I hope one day I can be like Imam Ali (AS). I am going to try my best to start concentrating in my prayers from today." Mrs. Hudda overheard Yasir and a delicate smile formed on her face. She raised her hands and prayed to the Almighty to always guide her students to the right path and to  let them be amongst those who are closest to Him.

Use this page to jot down anything you learned and that you think you can apply to your life.

Generosity
Lady Fatema (A.S)

It seemed like things in Class 786 were getting a bit better. The children seemed to be enjoying their adventures with Mrs. Hudda and things were improving slowly. However, occasionally the students' wild sides would pop out, and today just happened to be one of those days.

Mrs. Hudda opened the door of the classroom only to find it in an unbelievable mess. The students were running around and jumping up and down. Some were standing, others were sitting at their desks, and there were a few sitting on the halaqa rug trying to have a discussion. Across the halaqa rug, Mrs. Hudda heard Fizza and Zainab fighting about some markers.

"You CANNOT take MY stuff without MY permission!" scolded Fizza.

"OK Fizza, so can I *pleeeeeaaaseeeee* borrow it for a little while?" Zainab questioned sarcastically. "NO! I just got it yesterday and you are going to ruin it!" retorted Fizza. Feeling insulted, Zainab stuck out her tongue, rolled her eyes, and walked away.

Mrs. Hudda started to skip towards the bookshelf. The kids all started smiling and laughing. Her skipping make everyone forget what they were doing, and they all came to skip behind her and headed to the bookshelf. "She is definitely the coolest teacher we have ever had!" Ammar whispered to Yasir, as they quickly got on their feet and followed the other kids, who were already surrounding Mrs. Hudda. Curiosity was written all over their faces. The kids watched anxiously as Mrs. Hudda scanned the bookshelf.

Which of the amazing personalities were they going to learn about today?

Mrs. Hudda reached towards the books and took out a book titled "Hadith al-Kisa." The kids guessed, "Lady Fatema!" in unison.

"You are quite an intelligent bunch." Mrs. Hudda smiled. "Let's start with getting to know who Lady Fatema is."

"The daughter of the Holy Prophet!" Hadi blurted out.

"And the wife of Imam Ali!" exclaimed Sayyada.

"And the mother of Imam Hassan and Hussain!" shouted Shabbir.

"That's great! But what about her personality? What made *her* so special?"

"I don't know," Fizza responded timidly.

Mrs. Hudda had a mysterious look on her face and a twinkle in her eyes. Everyone in the class knew what that meant...it was time to travel back to the past! "Another adventure!" screamed Jawaad, jumping up with excitement.

As the rest of the children joined Jawaad in his excitement, Fizza rushed to her desk and quickly hid her markers in her backpack. She then joined the class for the adventure that awaited them.

LaBayk ya iMaM, LaBayk ya iMaM!

The blessed words bounced off the classroom walls as the children eagerly put their hands on the Hadith al-Kisa book. Fizza noticed a small triangular clay piece with the word 'Generosity' engraved on it fall out of the book. She grabbed it and put it in her purse pocket. The book began to glow and in the blink of an eye, the children found themselves in Medina. "Where are we?" asked Yasir, looking wary.

Before anybody could answer, the children heard footsteps and diverted their attention to a man wearing dirty, worn out clothes, crying out to anybody who would listen, "I'm hungry…look at what I'm wearing. Somebody please listen to me, please help me."

The poor man was begging door to door, pleading for help. Was anybody going to help him, the children wondered sadly. As the man approached one particular house, Mrs. Hudda told the children that that was no ordinary house, but the house of the Lady of Light, Lady Fatema.

Eager to get a peek, the children tried to get closer to the house. As they did, they saw the door of the house closing and the poor man walking away with a smile on his face and a beautiful necklace in his hand.

"Lady Fatema…" the poor man thought out aloud, "I have heard that she does not turn anybody away empty-handed and it is true. Look at this necklace! I can sell it to buy food and clothes for myself."

Mrs. Hudda, seeing the joy in the kids, instructed them to follow the beggar. The kids followed the beggar inquisitively.

The children saw an elderly man and his servant approaching the beggar. The man seemed to have recognized the necklace in the beggar's hand. He stopped him and politely introduced himself:

"Oh man, I am Ammar son of Yasir and I wish to buy the necklace you have with you. Would you be willing to sell it for 300 dirhams?"

"300 dirhams? How many dollars is that?" Asiya asked rummaging through her purse, "I would give all my pocket-money for a beautiful necklace like that!"

The beggar sold the necklace to Ammar for 300 dirhams. The beggar then went on to the market and bought food, clothes, and a horse for himself.

"This necklace belongs to Lady Fatema," Ammar told his young servant. "Return it to her and tell her that I have gifted the necklace and you to her."

Although sweaty and exhausted from their jogging, the children eagerly followed the young servant to the house of Lady Fatema (AS). The young boy gently knocked on the door and said, "My lady, Ammar has gifted this necklace and me to you!" From behind the door, Lady Fatema (AS) took the necklace and thanked the boy for returning it to her. She then freed the servant!

"Isn't that amazing?!" wondered Asiya. "How one generous act benefitted so many people!"

"One generous act of Lady Fatema (AS) got a poor man some food, clothes and a horse, and it also freed a slave!" Mrs. Hudda repeated.

"And she got her necklace back!" Fizza quickly added. "Do you always get back what you give in the way of Allah SWT?" questioned Asiya.

"Most definitely!" Mrs. Hudda assured her. "In fact, Allah SWT returns what you give in his way many times over – both in this world and the next!" Fizza, on realizing the importance of generosity, looked down with embarrassment. She remembered the way she had treated Zainab in the classroom.

As the children fell into silence, thinking about what they had just seen, the Hadith al-Kisa book started glowing again. Before they realized it, they found themselves in the same place but at a different time. It was evening, about Maghrib time.

Mrs. Hudda broke the silence by explaining the scenario of the next incident they were about to witness: "The two sons of Lady Fatema (AS), Imam Hassan and Imam Hussain (AS), were once very ill. Lady Fatema (AS) had promised Allah SWT that if He cured them and made them better, she would fast for three days. When Imam Ali (AS) found out about her promise, he also decided to promise to fast with her. When Imam Hassan, Imam Hussain (AS) and Lady Fizza found out, they too decided to join in on the fasting."

"By the Blessings of the Almighty, the young Imams got better and today Lady Fatema (AS) and her whole family are fasting." She continued, "It is now iftaar time and the family is preparing to break their fasts."

"Ssshhh!" Ammar tried to calm everyone down. "Look…there is another man begging for food," said Zainab sadly. "Poor man, he looks like he hasn't eaten for days," Aliya added.

The poor man knocked on the door of Lady Fatema (AS), saying, "I know you will not turn me away empty handed. Oh, Daughter of the Prophet, I am hungry, please give me something to eat."

"These loaves of bread are all I have. You can take them" Lady Fatema(AS) said, handing all she had for the family's iftaar to the beggar. Mrs. Hudda explained to the children that when Lady Fatema (AS) took her loaf to give to the poor man, everyone insisted that they wanted to give theirs away as well.

"She gave it all away! What are they going to have for iftaar?" Hadi asked with concern. Peeping through a tiny window, the children noticed that the family broke their fast with only water and salt. Yet they seemed happy, content, and grateful for Allah SWT's blessings.

The children continued to witness the same event over three days. On the second day, an orphan came to the house of Lady Fatema (AS). Just like the previous day, she and her family gave away all that they had for iftaar to the orphan. A similar incident happened again on the third day. This time, it was an innocent prisoner looking for help. The family of Lady Fatema (AS) did the exact same thing again. They gave away all they had for iftaar to the prisoner.

"Wow! Three days without food? Just having water and salt for iftaar?!" Fizza exclaimed, astonished. "I definitely wouldn't be able to do that! We need a halaqa session!" Hadi exclaimed in admiration.

The children gathered around in a circle to form their halaqa for discussion. Fizza started the discussion: "I think I have learned to think about others before I think about myself."

"Yes," added Hadi, "I think keeping your promises, regardless of the circumstances, is very important too. Lady Fatema (AS) and her family promised that if her two sons got well, they would fast. Even though it was so difficult, they kept their promise."

As the children shared their concerns about the family of Lady Fatema (AS) being hungry for three days, they noticed the house being covered by a beautiful glow. Mrs. Hudda explained to the children that Allah SWT was so pleased with their actions that He sent food from the heavens for Lady Fatema (AS) and her family. "And there is also a verse in the Qur'an in Surah Dahr, verse 8 which talks about this sacrifice that Lady Fatema (AS) and her family made," Mrs. Hudda added.

وَيُطْعِمُونَ الطَّعَامَ عَلَىٰ حُبِّهِ

And they feed for the love of Allah,

مِسْكِينًا وَيَتِيمًا وَأَسِيرًا

the needy, the orphan, and the captive

The kids wondered where they were going to go next when the Hadith al-Kisa book started glowing again. Their surrounding began to change and they were taken into a corner of a small house. Looking out of the window, Mrs. Hudda asked the children, "Can you see the Prophet (SAW)? That's him coming towards Lady Fatema (AS)'s house." At that point, the children were surprised to realize that they were actually in the house of Lady Fatema (AS).

The Holy Prophet Muhammed (SAW) entered his daughter's house and said, "Oh my daughter Fatema, peace be upon you. I am not feeling too well today; I am going to lie down for a while. Could you please bring me the Yemeni blanket?"

Lady Fatema (AS) responded:

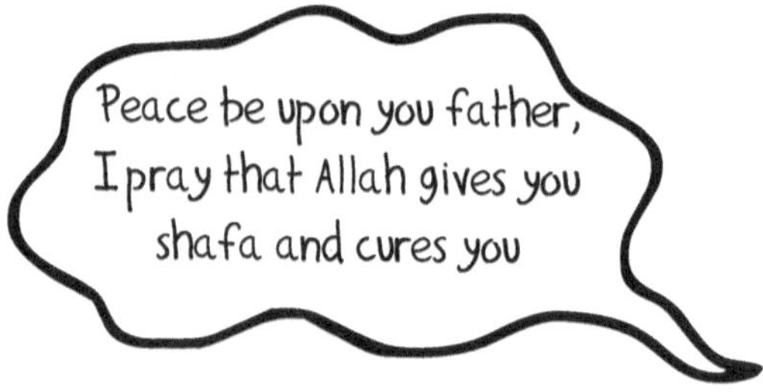

Lady Fatema (AS) got the blanket and covered her father with it. As she wrapped it around him, his face shone like a full moon with all its glory and splendor.

A few minutes later, there was a knock at the door. Imam Hassan (AS) entered saying: "Oh mother, peace be upon you. I can smell the sweet and pure fragrance of my grandfather, The Holy Prophet of Allah."

Lady Fatema (AS) responded:

Imam Hassan (AS) walked over to the blanket, greeted his grandfather and asked him, "May I join you under the blanket?"

The Holy Prophet Muhammed (SAW) answered, "Yes my son, Oh the Master of the Fountain of Kawther, you may join me underneath the blanket."

A few minutes later, there was another knock on the door of Lady Fatema (AS)'s house. Imam Hussain (AS) entered and said, "Oh mother, peace be upon you. I smell the sweet and pure fragrance of my grandfather, the Holy Prophet of Allah SWT."

Lady Fatema (AS) responded:

Imam Hussain (AS) walked over to the blanket and said, "Oh grandfather, the chosen of Allah, peace be upon you. May I join you under the blanket?"

The Holy Prophet Muhammed (SAW) answered "Oh Hussain, peace be upon you too, oh my son, the one who will be the intercessor for the believers. You may join me."

A little while later there was another knock on the door. Imam Ali (AS) entered and said, "Oh Fatema, peace be upon you. I smell the sweet and pure fragrance of my cousin, The Holy Prophet"

Lady Fatema(AS) responded:

Imam Ali (AS) walked over to the blanket and after greeting the Prophet (SAW) said, "Oh Prophet of Allah, may I join you under the blanket?"

The Prophet (SAW) responded, "Peace be upon you too, oh Ali, my brother, my successor and my standard bearer. Yes, Ali you may join me under the blanket."

Soon after, Lady Fatema (AS) walked over to the blanket and asked:

The Holy Prophet Muhammed (SAW) responded, "Oh my daughter, oh the one who is a part of me. You may also come underneath the blanket."

The children watched as the Holy Prophet (SAW) raised the blanket towards the heavens and prayed to Allah SWT, "Oh Allah, these are the people of my family. They are my supporters. Their flesh is my flesh and their blood is my blood. Whoever loves them loves me, whoever hurts them hurts me. They are from me and I am from them!"

Soon after, Allah SWT sent down angel Jibrail, who also wanted to join them underneath the blanket. Angel Jibrail asked for permission to enter, and when it was granted, he told the Holy Prophet (SAW), "The Almighty has asked me to tell you that He has created the entire universe with all of its beauties, only out of the love for the people under this blanket - you and your family."

The Holy Prophet (SAW) then said, "By the Almighty who has made me His Prophet, I swear that whoever recites this story when they get together, they have the mercy of the Almighty Allah on them. The angels will descend to ask for forgiveness on their behalf and their wishes will be fulfilled, as well as their grief and troubles removed..."

The children's eyes began to water. They had never realized how beautiful the story of the blanket was. They remembered that it was always recited at the mosque, but they had never understood what it meant. "LABAYK YA IMAM," Mrs. Hudda whispered, signalling to the class that it was time to head back to class. They followed her lead, put their hands on the book, and repeated the words.

The children found themselves back in their classroom. Sayyada glanced at the wall clock and the calendar. They had only been gone for 45 minutes! Everyone gathered around the halaqa rug for the end of class discussion.

Asiya asked Mrs. Hudda if she could share a story with the class. When the teacher gave her the permission, she started speaking. "One day the Holy Prophet (SAW) noticed Lady Fatema (AS) working very hard and decided to give her a gift. He told her to recite Allahu Akber (Allah is the Greatest) 34 times, Alhamdulillah (All praise is for Allah) 33 times, and SubhanAllah (Glory be to Allah) 33 times and end with La illah illalah (There is no God but Allah). He instructed her to recite it after each wajib salaat and before she went to sleep."

Fizza, in deep thought, cringed her face and blurted out, "That's the Tasbih of Lady Fatema (AS)! The one we recite after praying all the time!"

"Our prayer is like a beautiful flower," Mrs. Hudda began to explain. "The Tasbih of Lady Fatema (AS) that we do after each prayer adds fragrance, a beautiful smell, to that flower. Without doing the Tasbih of Lady Fatema (AS), we are presenting a flower to Allah SWT that has no smell."

"So we should always do Tasbih of Lady Fatema (AS) after our salaat," suggested Hadi.

"What an amazing gift Lady Fatema (AS) passed on to us!" exclaimed Fizza.

The children made a resolution that from then onwards, they would always remember to do the tasbih after their prayers. They took out their notepads and started writing down the facts about Lady Fatema (AS).

Name: Fatema

Title: Sayyidatun Nisa Al-alaameen (The Leader of the Women of the Universe)

Birthdate: 20th Jamaadil Aakhar 615 AD

Mother: Lady Khadijah

Father: Holy Prophet Muhammed

Married: Imam Ali

Children: Imam Hassan, Imam Hussain, Lady Zainab, Lady Umm Kulthum and Mohsin, who died in her womb when the enemies broke down her door on her.

Died: 3rd of Jamaadil Aakhar at the age of 18

Burial place: Buried in secret

While everyone was busy writing, Fizza pulled Zainab aside. "I am really sorry for being mean to you and not sharing my new markers with you," Fizza told Zainab. "I learned from Lady Fatema (AS) that you should always be generous. I hope you can forgive me. Here," she continued, taking out her markers, "you can borrow them for the next class."

"That's okay, Fizza. Thank you for letting me borrow them. I promise I will take good care of them. I too should have asked politely. I am also sorry" replied Zainab with a warm smile, "and you can use my new markers too."

The two girls hugged each other and started making their way to their next class, afraid that the tardy bell might beat them.

Before leaving, Fizza took out the triangular piece that said 'Generosity' and wore it around her neck to remind her to always be generous and giving.

Mrs. Hudda sat down peacefully on the worn out, wooden chair, and started reciting Hadith al-Kisa.

Use this page to jot down anything you learned and that you think you can apply to your life.

Peace
& Anger
Management
Imam Hassan (A.S)

As everyone started getting ready for class after recess, they noticed a disappointed Mr. Hashim coming towards Class 786. He had with him two sweaty and bruised boys, his hand firmly gripping each boy by the shoulder. Upon seeing the inquisitive look on Mrs. Hudda's face, he went on to relate the events of the afternoon and told her that he had found the two boys fighting at the soccer field. Ignoring the conversation taking place between the teacher and the principal, the two boys, Haydar and Jawaad, continued bickering.

"Haydar called me a nasty name!" cried Jawaad. "No I did not! I was only being honest when I called you dumb!" retorted Haydar.

Mr. Hashim had had enough of the quarrel. He was at his wits end and had tried everything from detention to suspension, but nothing had worked. He walked out of the room leaving Mrs. Hudda to deal with the two mischief-makers.

The two boys began to fight again. Jawaad tried to punch Haydar but Mrs. Hudda broke them up before the fight could go any further. She gave the two boys a stern look and they instantly stopped bickering. She then turned her attention to the rest of the class and had that mysterious twinkle in her eyes. With excitement, the class yelled "FIELD TRIP!" Mrs. Hudda led the children to the class library and began rummaging through the books. Finally, she pulled out an old brown parched scroll. The class was curious and started questioning what this odd-looking piece of paper was and where it came from.

Be quiet or I will give you all bloody noses!" threatened Jawaad who was still writhing with anger. Mrs. Hudda calmed Jawaad down and gave him that stern look again. She warned him that if he continued to behave that way and didn't restrain his anger, he would not be able to join the rest of the class on their special field trip.

Pointing to the ancient looking document, she continued, "This was the treaty that Imam Hassan (AS) signed with Muawiyah which has played a very important role in Islam."

She told them to put their hands on the scroll and say the blessed words. A triangular clay piece fell out of the scroll and Jawaad quickly picked it up. The piece read 'Peace and Anger Management'. He put it in his pocket and joined the class in saying:

"LABAYK YA IMAM"

A few moments later, the children found themselves in the house of the second Imam, Imam Hassan (AS), who was preparing to eat a meal. All the students stood quietly, awe stricken by the sight of their second Imam.

CRASH!! The class jumped at the sound of a glass breaking. They turned around to see a maid standing still, shivering out of fear. She had just dropped a bowl of hot soup on the Imam.

Jawaad's eyes widened. "Oh, he's going to get SO mad at her!" he said.

"Ssshhhh Jawaad, he is not like you!" Haydar blurted out. Mrs. Hudda looked at both of them and gave them a silent warning.

Instantly, the maid began to recite the first part of verse 134 of Surah Ale-Imran of the Holy Qur'an:

"وَالْكَاظِمِينَ الْغَيْظَ

Those who control their anger"

"I am not angry," replied Imam Hassan (AS) in a very calm voice. Upon hearing this, Jawaad heaved a sigh of disappointment. "Ah! I was hoping for more drama and excitement!"

The maid then recited the next part of the verse:

وَالْعَافِينَ عَنِ النَّاسِ ۗ

And are forgiving towards people

"I have already forgiven you," added Imam Hassan (AS).

She then read the last part of the verse:

وَاللَّهُ يُحِبُّ الْمُحْسِنِينَ

And Allah loves those who do good

"You are free and no longer my servant," Imam Hassan (AS) informed her.

Jawaad frowned and wrinkles formed on his forehead. He began thinking about how Imam Hassan (AS) did not get angry with the maid for spilling hot soup on him. What surprised Jawaad even more was the fact that Imam Hassan (AS) forgave his maid and freed her even though she had made the mistake! "I wonder how he is able to control his anger? If I was him I would be so ready to pound someone!" Jawaad thought out loud.

In the meantime, Mrs. Hudda began ushering the kids out of the house. Jawaad was standing still, deeply engrossed in his thoughts. He was ready to snap when Mrs. Hudda told him to hurry up. Mrs. Hudda noticed Jawaad's fury and patted his shoulders and smiled at him. Jawaad tried to swallow his anger and they continued to walk with the rest of the children.

The children were roaming the streets of Medina when they saw Imam Hassan (AS) again. They also noticed a Syrian horse-rider approaching the Imam. As the Syrian got closer to Imam Hassan (AS), the children heard him insulting the Imam.

Jawaad muttered "not this time!" under his breath. He didn't think the Imam would let this Syrian man go without teaching him a lesson or two! Jawaad was surprised to see the Imam keeping calm and saying nothing at all.

When the Syrian finally slowed down and stopped his insults, Imam Hassan (AS) walked over to him and cheerfully greeted the man and said, "Old man, I believe you are a stranger. Maybe you have confused me with another person. If you ask forgiveness, it is granted to you. If you ask for a means of transportation, we shall provide it for you. If you are hungry, we shall feed you. If you are in need of clothes, we shall clothe you. If you are deprived, we shall grant you. If you are being sought, we shall give you refuge. If you have any need, we shall fulfill it for you. And if you wish to proceed with your caravan to be our guest until you leave, it would be more useful to you, for we hold a good position, great dignity, and vast knowledge."

"No way!" exclaimed Sayyada.

"I think my mom forgot to clean out my ears today! I must have heard him wrong!" stuttered Shabbir.

The entire class stared at Imam Hassan (AS) in awe. It seemed that they were not alone because, by the look on his face, the Syrian man was also taken aback. He stood speechless after hearing the response of Imam Hassan (AS).

He turned to the Imam saying, "I testify that you are Allah's vicegerent on this earth. Allah surely knows who He gives His message to. When I entered this city, you and your father were the most hated of Allah's creatures to me, but now you are the most beloved of Allah's creatures to me."

Jawaad's jaw dropped in disbelief at the effect kind words could have on such an arrogant man. Imam Hassan (AS) truly practiced what he preached. The children saw the effects of being good to those who are mean to you. Mrs. Hudda prayed the children's hearts would accept these lessons they are learning and adopt the ways of our Masumeen.

Suddenly the surroundings changed. The children found themselves near a marketplace. Once again, they spotted Imam Hassan (AS) in the streets of Medina, this time he was heading towards what looked like the marketplace. Mrs. Hudda urged them to follow along. "Where are we going? My feet hurt!" complained Asiya.

"I told you to wear your sneakers instead of those fancy red sandals!" snickered Hadi.

Mrs. Hudda interrupted the two and informed the class that they had almost reached their destination.

Walking on, the students realized that what looked like the marketplace was something like a public meeting hall. They noticed a crowd of men gathered there. As soon as Imam Hassan (AS) drew closer to the crowd, a handful of men started pointing towards him and shouting, it seemed as if they had been waiting for him. The children noticed that Imam Hassan (AS) was holding a scroll that looked very similar to the one that they had used to travel back to the past.

"Hmmm, that looks so familiar. I wonder where we saw that before Mrs. Hudda" Yasir joked. Mrs. Hudda and the class all giggled. They watched as Imam Hassan (AS) walked towards the crowd and opened the parchment he was holding in his hands.

He explained to the crowd that in his hand was a peace treaty, signed by Muawiyah and himself.

"Muawiyah!" gasped Asiya. "He was a very evil man"

"What's the peace treaty all about?" questioned Hadi.

"I think if we all stop talking and listen to what Imam Hassan (AS) has to say, we might find out what the treaty is all about, don't you think?" Jawaad questioned sarcastically.

"Muawiyah has agreed to the following terms," they heard the Imam say, explaining the contents of the treaty to the people of Medina.

"Wow, I never thought Muawiyah could make and keep promises! I guess they have it in writing and that's all that matters!" Ammar wondered out loud.

"That's true Ammar, you know what they say - think twice before it's in black and white. He now has no choice but to keep the promises," agreed Zainab.

1. Muawiyah should rule strictly according to the Holy Qur'an and the example of the Holy Prophet (SAW).

2. Muawiyah should not appoint or nominate anyone to be the ruler after him but it should go back to the Ahlul Bayt, the family of the Prophet who are the rightful successors.

3. The people should be left in peace, wherever they are in the land of Allah

4. The harassment of the companions of Imam Ali (AS) should immediately be stopped; their lives and properties and families guaranteed safe conduct and peace.

5. The cursing of Imam Ali (AS) from the mimbar (pulpit) should stop immediately.

6. No harm should be done secretly or openly against Imam Hassan (AS) and his brother Imam Hussain (AS), or any of the Ahlul Bayt."

Mrs. Hudda told the class that from the very beginning, Muawiyah never kept the promises he had made in the treaty. Soon after signing the treaty, he trampled on his copy of the treaty and said, "Do you think I have taken power to teach you about Islam? No, I have taken power for the sake of it. And if anyone tries to disagree with me, they shall pay a costly price of losing their head!"

The children stared at Mrs. Hudda in astonishment as she narrated what happened after the peace treaty was signed.

Mrs. Hudda then continued to explain that Muawiyah was successful in keeping the power of the throne within his family by nominating his son, Yazid, as the ruler of the kingdom after him.

"Yazid! I can't stand the thought of him! He is scum!" Jawaad said disgustedly.

"Yes, Jawaad, May Allah SWT not be pleased with him. In this case, you can definitely express your anger. It's okay to feel anger towards the oppressors."

The students all crowded around Mrs. Hudda as she held out the scroll. They all put a finger on the scroll and said "LABAYK YA IMAM!"

In a split second, the students were back in the classroom. Before Mrs. Hudda could tell them that it was halaqa time, the children all rushed to the halaqa rug.

They eagerly formed a circle and took out their notepads to write down what they had learnt and the facts about Imam Hassan (AS) that Mrs. Hudda was writing on the chalk board.

<u>Imam Hassan (AS) was very kind and did not get angry with people even when they were mean to him. I am going to try to say nice words to my little sister.</u>

Name : Hassan

Title : Al-Mujtabah
        (The Chosen One)

Birthdate : 15 Ramadhan, 3 A.H

Mother : Lady Fatema

Father : Imam Ali

Children : All of his sons were
killed in Kerbala except one who
was called Hassan al-Muthana

Died : Either 7th or 28th Safar,
       50 A.H. aged 47.

Burial place : In Jannatul Baqi in
                Medina

"Mrs. Hudda, how was Imam Hassan (AS) martyred?" questioned Asiya curiously.

"Muawiyah tried to kill Imam Hassan (AS) seven times," Mrs. Hudda began to explain. "He was successful in his last attempt because he convinced Jo'dah bint Ashath – the wife of the Imam – to poison him. She fell for Muawiyah's trap because he had promised her that he would marry her to his son, Yazid. However, after she poisoned the Imam, Muawiyah backed out and refused to marry her to Yazid. He said to her that if she was capable of killing a pious man like the Imam, she was definitely capable of killing Yazid."

There was silence in the classroom as everyone thought about the sad event of Imam Hassan's death. Suddenly, Jawaad broke the silence by asking Mrs. Hudda if he could lead the discussion. After Mrs. Hudda nodded in approval, Jawaad took a deep breath and started. "I learnt that Imam Hassan (AS) was awesome at controlling his anger. I realized that as a Muslim, it is important not to get angry easily over petty things and to swallow your anger when it wants to bubble out... I get angry easily but because of what I learnt today from Imam Hassan (AS), I now know it is not right and whenever I get angry, I will inshAllah think of Imam Hassan (AS)'s actions and try to swallow my anger. I also learned that's its okay to be angry with the enemies of the Ahlul Bayt, and the oppressors. It's important to be able to think of the right reasons to be angry."

Mrs. Hudda gave Jawaad a gentle smile and helped him wear the triangular piece which had 'Peace and Anger Management' engraved on it. Jawaad looked at the triangular piece and said that he would always keep it with him like a good-luck charm.

The children were so engrossed in the discussion that no one noticed Mr. Hashim standing at the door. He watched as Jawaad got up and started walking towards Haydar. "Here we go again," Mr. Hashim sighed in disappointment, anticipating the quarrel to start all over.

"Yo bro, I am really sorry for punching you on the nose. I am sorry for letting my anger get the better of me and for bursting out at you."

Mr. Hashim lifted his eyebrow, stunned. Noticing Mrs. Hudda smiling at him, he cleared his throat and walked out quietly.

Haydar and Jawad decided to sign a peace

treaty with each other. They decided that Jawaad wouldn't get angry and Haydar wouldn't call him names anymore. They both looked at each other and promised not to be like Muawiyah. No matter what came their way, they would do their best to keep the promises they made to each other in their treaty!

Use this page to jot down anything you learned and that you think you can apply to your life.

Sacrifice
Imam Hussain (A.S)

Zzzzzzz... The sounds of Taha snoring away filled Class 786 as Sheikh Hussam babbled away. You could see 'boredom' written all over the students' faces.

Just as Sheikh Hussam came to the end of his lecture, he heard Taha's snores.

Walking over to the back of the room where Taha was drooling and snoring, Sheikh Hussam jerked Taha awake. "Wake up, you rude little boy! You like to sleep in my class, huh? Now that you are well rested, get up and run 5 laps around the entire soccer field, without stopping for a drink!"

Taha, with sleepy and yet fearful eyes, ran out of the classroom. After he was done with the 5 laps, he came back to the classroom, exhausted.

"Look at you, all sweaty, tired, and exhausted! Now you will never fall asleep in my class," yelled Sheikh Hussam.

"Ding Ding Ding Ding!!" rang the bell at Al-Iman Madrassah. Sheikh Hussam started packing up, and reminded the class of the 25 page homework assignment due the next week.

Mrs. Hudda had arrived a little early for class that day. Having observed the last 5 minutes of Sheik Hussam's class, she thought to herself, "No wonder these kids act up like that. I would go nuts if I had to deal with that." She entered the classroom, looked at Taha sympathetically and began giving out candy to the entire class. "YES! chocolate is my favorite…" Imran commented as his mouth began to water.

"Mrs. Hudda, why are we getting candy?" Asiya asked.

"Hey dummy, don't ask. Just take it and be happy!" retorted Taha, trying to take his frustration out at Asiya.

"Taha, can we calm down please?" asked Mrs. Hudda gently.

Turning towards the rest of the class, she continued to answer Asiya's question. "The candy is for the mawlood celebration for the next 3 days. It is the birthday of Imam Hussain (AS), Hazrat Abul Faadhil Abbas (AS), and Imam Zain-ul-Abideen (A.S)."

The children saw the mysterious twinkle in Mrs. Hudda's eyes as she walked towards the bookshelf. This time she took out a book titled "Ziyarat Ashura." The children were very familiar with the Ziyarat. It was the same Ziyarat that they recited with the community on every Ashura to send salaams on Imam Hussain (AS).

"Ziyarat Ashura!" exclaimed Taha. "Is that not directly sent from Allah SWT? The Ziyarat cursing the killers of Imam Hussain (AS)? My mom said that if you have faith, this Ziyarat can change your life and work miracles!"

"That's right Taha, this Ziyarat is the word of Allah SWT. If you recite Ziyarat Ashura when you are in danger or really need help, Allah SWT will definitely help you out" Mrs. Hudda responded. "Time to travel children... you know the drill" she added with a laugh!

They all placed their hands on the book and repeated together,

Taha quickly grabbed the small triangular piece that fell out of the book. He read the word "Sacrifice" engraved on it and put it in his pocket. Before the children knew it, they were zapped into…

"Where on earth are we?" Aliya asked, surprised. Looking around at the clouds surrounding them, Sabira responded, "Good question…I don't think we're on earth!"

"Whoa! This is way too much for me. I am scared of heights and flying! Hold on! How did we get up here?" shrieked Hadi.

"OUCH!" screamed Sayyada, as she felt a sharp pain. "Sorry," Fizza whispered. "I was just making sure this wasn't a dream."

"You are supposed to pinch yourself, not me!" snapped Sayyada.

They were taken by surprise when it dawned on them that they were on the wings of a huge creature. Looking confused, they looked over to Mrs. Hudda for an answer. She informed them that they were on the wings of Angel Jibrail, who had been commanded by Allah SWT to lead a group of angels to visit the house of the Holy Prophet Muhammed (SAW). The children were about to ask why they were going to the Prophet (SAW)'s house when they got distracted by the sight of the angels following Jibrail. They tried to count the number of angels but there were too many of them! The sight was absolutely overwhelming.

Taha started scratching his back vigorously searching for something. "Why don't I have wings?"

Mrs. Hudda laughed and told him that he was born human. "Humans don't have wings Taha, but they can definitely fly higher than the angels according to their level of faith in Allah SWT."

When they got to the house of Lady Fatema (AS), they saw Lady Fatema (AS) give the Holy Prophet Muhammed (SAW) a baby, it was Imam Hussain (AS). The Holy Prophet whilst holding baby Imam Hussain (AS) in his arms, recited the Adhan and Iqamah in his tiny ears.

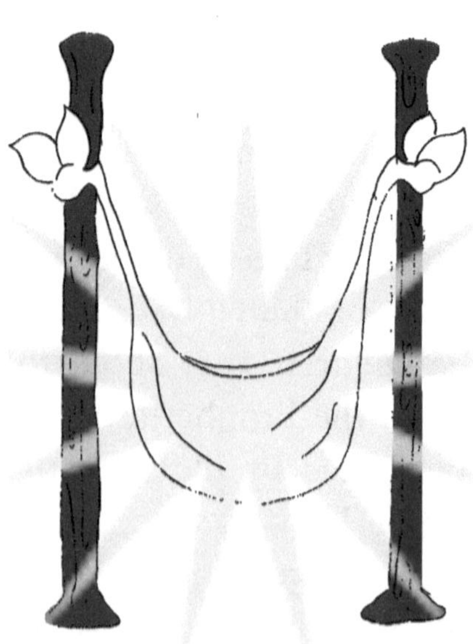

The children's eyes were watering. This was such a beautiful moment. They saw how special this baby was, and how the inhabitants of the heavens and the earths were celebrating this birth.

Just then Yasir noticed that the Holy Prophet (SAW) also had tears in his eyes.

Mrs. Hudda, "Shouldn't Prophet Muhammed (SAW) be happy? Those don't look like tears of joy" Yasir shared.

Before Mrs. Hudda could explain, they heard Lady Fatema (AS) asking the Holy Prophet (SAW) why he was shedding tears. The Prophet (SAW) told her, that Angel Jibrail informed him that this baby in his hands will be killed. Lady Fatema (AS) also had tears in her eyes when she heard that.

Shabbir and Fizza gasped. Why would anyone dare to kill such a special baby, the grandson of the Holy Prophet and the son of the Lady of Light and Ameerul Momineen? The children were all complaining to Mrs. Hudda. They couldn't believe that some people would kill this special grandson of the Prophet. They had the same blood, why would they harm him. Mrs. Hudda told them to have patience and they will see how history unfolds.

Before they left, they saw Prophet Muhammed (SAW) consoling his daughter. He told her not to worry, for there will be a nation of people who will weep over the tragedy of Kerbala until the Day of Judgment. The children also felt comforted knowing they were a part of that nation. Even though they didn't understand the tragedy of Kerbala fully, they still shed tears for Imam Hussain (AS) every Ashura. It just came naturally.

The book of Ziyarat Ashura in Mrs. Hudda's hand started to glow and all the kids touched it. Before they knew it, they were no longer at the house of the Prophet (SAW), but instead at a mosque a number of years later, where they saw Imam Hussain (AS) – as an adult - just finishing a prayer. They listened as Imam Hussain (AS) talked to an Arab man.

The Arab man asked the Imam a question. "I disobey Allah SWT and cannot stop myself from sins. Therefore, please give me some advice, Oh son of the Prophet, so that I may keep away from sins."

After hearing this, Taha and the rest of the children start remembering the times when they had disobeyed Allah SWT.

"You can commit as many sins as you want if you can do any of the five things I ask you to" Imam Hussain (AS) told the Arab Man.

"Please tell me what these 5 things are," requested the man.

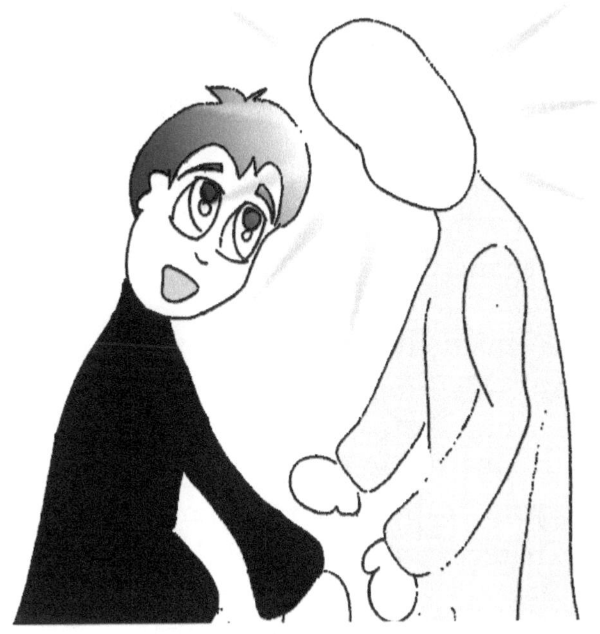

"*Firstly*, do not eat from the provisions of Allah SWT, and then do whatever you like," began Imam Hussain (AS).

"Then what will I eat, because whatever is in this universe is from Allah SWT?!" replied the man.

"*Secondly*, leave the universe of Allah SWT and then do whatever you like. Find a place that Allah SWT does not own, and then you are free to sin," continued Imam Hussain (AS).

Everyone was astonished because they knew it was impossible to leave Allah SWT's universe. "This is even more difficult than the first!" exclaimed the man. "If I leave the universe, then where could I go? Everything belongs to Allah!"

"*Then* find a place where Allah SWT cannot see you, then do whatever you like," the Imam continued again.

"But O Imam Hussain (AS), nothing is hidden from Allah SWT," replied the man.

"*Then* do one thing: when the Angel of Death comes to you, keep him away from yourself, and then do whatever you like," said the Imam.

"It is not possible!" replied the man.

"If you cannot do any of those, *then* do not enter hell when Allah SWT sends you into it. If you can do that, then go and commit whatever sins you like."

The man then made a promise. "O son of the Prophet of Allah, from today Allah SWT will not find me in a situation which He dislikes!"

"That was quite a conversation!" said Hadi.

"Whoa, that really is cool! The lessons Imam Hussain (AS) just taught us can keep us away from ANY sin we would ever want to commit! If only we really reflected and pondered over our actions" said Aliya, thinking out loud.

Suddenly there was a loud thunder crash and the students found themselves in a dark night in the deserted plains.

"I love this time traveling! I wonder how Mrs. Hudda does it?!" Sayyada exclaimed.

The children could feel the hot winds of the desert hitting their faces. They could not even begin to imagine how hot the plains could get during the day. Taha remembered his thirst when Sheikh Hussam punished him and made him run 5 laps without stopping for a drink.

Mrs. Hudda informed the children that they had come to the land of Karbala – in the beginning of the year 61 AH. She took the children to the tent of Imam Hussain (AS) where some of his companions were reciting Qur'an, others were praying, and some were with their families, all preparing to give their lives and everything they had for the love of Allah SWT and Islam.

"This is the night of Ashura," whispered Aunali. They watched as Imam Hussain (AS) switched off the candles and asked his companions to leave if they wanted to survive. He told them that in the darkness nobody would know who left the camp and neither would it be something to be ashamed of. Not a single person moved. The companions insisted on staying with Imam Hussain (AS) until the very end.

On seeing this, tears trickled down from the tiny eyes of the students, down their soft cheeks like a calm waterfall.

The children's hearts were reaching out to Imam Hussain (AS). If only time had allowed them to be able to help Imam Hussain (AS).

"Labayk Ya Imam.. Here I am, O Imam… Labayk Ya Imam," each of them whispered.

Lightening struck the desert and the winds started to howl. Waves of the river Euphrates were hitting against the shores. After a while, there was absolute silence in the land of Kerbala. Mrs. Hudda explained to the students that it was now the day of Ashura, everything was destroyed and all the men, friends and family, of Imam Hussain (AS) had been martyred. The tents were in ashes and the orphaned children of Imam's family were sleeping on the desert sand, after having been slapped and their things taken away. Taha could not hold his tears back and he burst out crying. Looking around them, no one could resist crying. On that hard day, everything cried and mourned for Imam Hussain (AS) in its own unique way. The sun eclipsed, the stars were visible in the daylight, the fish wept. The skies wept blood and the wind howled because of the cruelty committed against the grandson of the Holy Prophet (SAW).

Mrs. Hudda took out the Ziyarat Ashura book and all the children gathered around her. They began reciting it together, sending their salaams to Imam Hussain (AS). They put their hands on the book and said "LABAYK YA IMAM" and were zapped back into their classroom at Al-Iman Madrassah. The children, still saddened by the event of Kerbala, took out their notebooks and sat quietly on the halaqa rug. The classroom was in absolute silence as everyone was recalling what they had just witnessed.

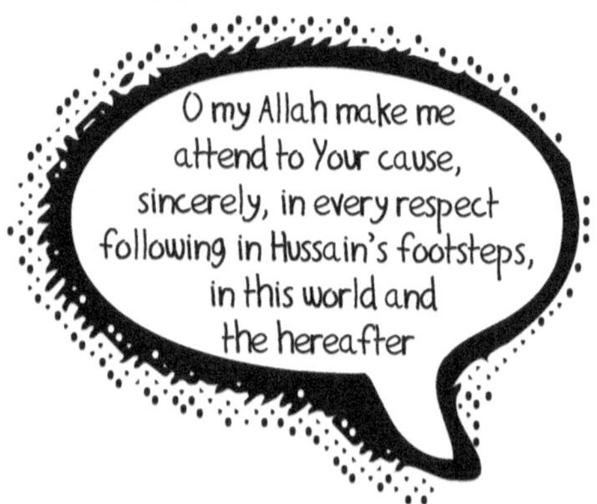

"I don't get it, if he was so special as a baby, then why would the Muslims in Karbala kill him?" Fizza asked.

"I think their hearts were so corrupt and black because of their sins that they didn't care about what they did, even though they knew it was wrong. It was as if a seal was placed on their hearts and they couldn't see what was right and wrong. They wanted money and power, not Allah SWT's pleasure!" answered Hadi with a tone of anger.

"They had their priorities wrong!"

"You know if we always remember the five things Imam Hussain told the Arab man, then InshAllah, with Allah's help, our hearts will never go bad," Yasir told the class. As Mrs. Hudda wrote some facts about Imam Hussain (AS) on the board, the children wrote them down in their notebooks.

Name: Hussain

Titles: Sayyed al- Shabaab Ahlil Jannah (The Leader of the Youth of Paradise) and Sayyed ash-Shohada (The Master of all the Martyrs)

Birthdate: 3rd Shabaan, 4 A.H.

Children: Imam Ali Zain-ul-Abideen (AS), Lady Fatema Kubra, Hazrat Ali Akber, Lady Fatema Sughra, Lady Sakina, and Hazrat Ali Asgher.

Martyred: On the 10th of Muharram, 61 A.H.

Taha stood up abruptly. "Labayk Ya Mahdi," he said firmly. "I don't know about you guys, but I hope that I will be a devoted companion of Imam Mahdi (AS) - like the people we saw in the tent of Imam Hussain (AS) who said they would give up everything for the love of Allah, the Imam and Islam."

He told the class that from that day onwards, his and everyone else's duty was to wait for the re-appearance of Imam Zamana (AJTF). While waiting, they needed to work hard to be the best Muslims they could be so that when he came, they could help him avenge the killing of Imam Hussain (AS).

"Who is Imam Zamana?" asked Asiya, looking confused.

No one heard her, as there was a loud uproar of "Al ajal Ya Mahdi, al ajal Ya Mahdi, come quick Imam Mahdi," in the class.

Taha pulled out the triangular piece that said 'Sacrifice' and wore it around his neck to remind him that saving Islam is important. Sometimes you have to give up things you like and make a few sacrifices for the reward of Allah SWT in the hereafter. Sacrifices like listening to a boring teacher, because he is teaching the word of Allah SWT and one can always learn!

"DING DING DING"

Al-Iman's bell sounded, signaling the end of class.

As everyone began leaving, Mrs. Hudda pulled Asiya aside. "Imam Zamana is the Imam of our time, Imam Mahdi (AS)," she whispered with a twinkle in her eyes. "And who knows, InshAllah we might just be blessed with the opportunity of being one of his companions."

Use this page to jot down anything you learned and that you think you can apply to your life.

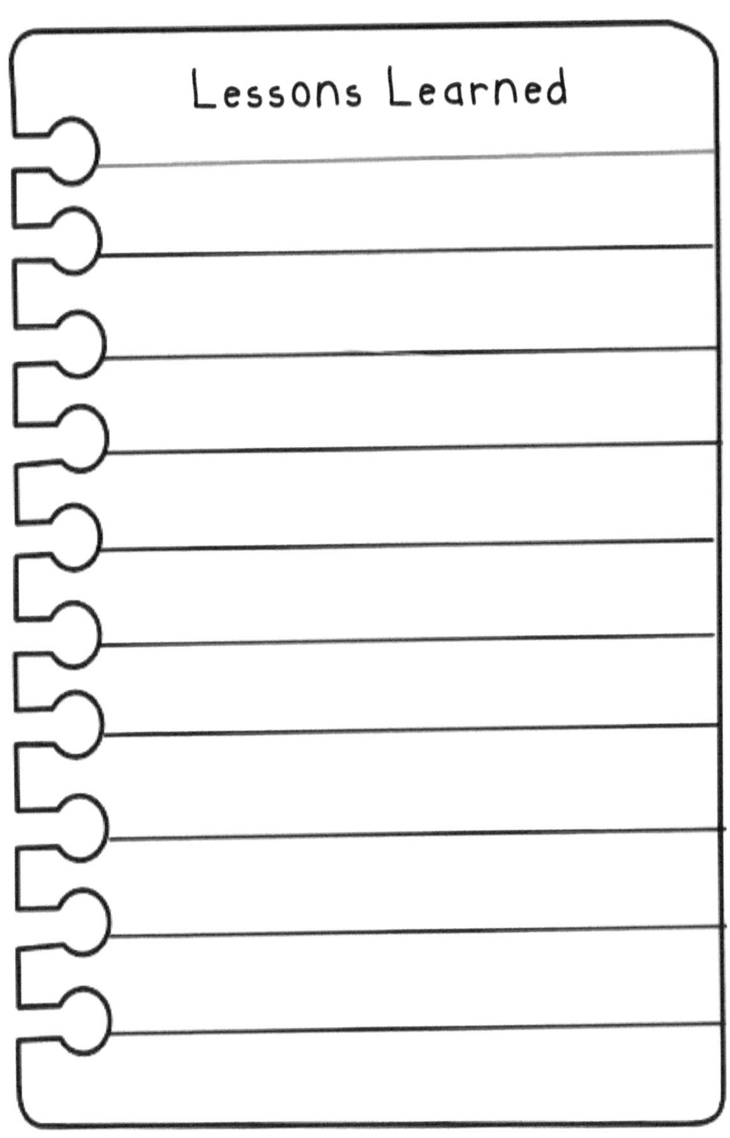

Du'a
Imam Zain
al-Abideen (A.S)

It was just minutes before class was supposed to begin. As Mrs. Hudda walked up the stairs, she saw students' of Al-Iman Madrassah rushing to their classrooms. The students of Class 786 however, were in no rush to make it to class before the tardy bell as they were already in their classroom. Mr. Hashim walked past Class 786 and was bewildered to see the naughtiest class so well-mannered and on time.

"These cannot be the same students! They aren't acting wild like they used to!" he thought to himself as he bumped into a student running to class.

"Listen guys!" Ammar shouted at the top of his lungs, trying to get everyone's attention. "Listen guys," he repeated, but only managed to get some giggles.

Mrs. Hudda walked into the classroom. As usual the children's eyes lit up when they saw her, knowing she had prepared an amazing adventure for them.

"Salaam Alaykum children" came her greeting, in her warm, caring, and gentle voice. "Alaykum Salaam Mrs. Hudda!" they responded eagerly, wondering where they would travel to today. Mrs. Hudda turned her attention to Ammar who looked like he was ready to burst. "Do you have something you would like to share with the class, Ammar?"

"I just wanted to tell everyone a story that my mom told me about the fourth Imam. He's quite an amazing guy!" Ammar explained.

"Yes he is, Ammar. As a matter of fact, today we are going learn a lot about him. Does anybody know the name of our fourth Imam?" questioned Mrs. Hudda. Aliya's hand sky-rocketed in to the air, "I do! His name is Ali but we usually call him by his title Imam Zain al-Abideen (AS)."

"That's right, Aliya. Well done. Did you know that the fourth Imam has left us a very special book? Does anybody know the name of that book? It is a book of prayers for all kinds of things. It has du'as for when you are sick, or travelling, and for many other things," said Mrs. Hudda.

Ammar could no longer control himself and shouted out, "Mrs. Hudda! My mom told me. The name of the book is Saheefa as-Sajjadiyya!"

Everyone watched as Mrs. Hudda pulled out the Saheefa as-Sajjadiyya from the book shelf, a beautiful blue book with gold writing.

The children walked over to the halaqa rug where Mrs. Hudda had gone to sit. She smiled at their enthusiasm and asked them to think of an event they had witnessed in their last adventure where the fourth Imam (AS) was present. Everyone put on their thinking caps, going back to the last time they had travelled into the past. Sayyada, with tears in her eyes, said in a very soft tone, "The fourth Imam was there in Kerbala, he is Imam Hussain (AS)'s son." "That's correct Sayyada. Today we will go to a time right after the tragedy of Kerbala, when the fourth Imam is the Imam of the time."

The children all rushed to put their hands on the Saheefa as-Sajjadiya and eagerly recited:

As the Saheefa illuminated the classroom, Ammar picked up a triangular piece that had fallen out of the Saheefa. It had the word 'Du'a' on it – which means supplication or prayer.

In a matter of seconds, the class was zapped back to a huge palace in Kufa. Mrs. Hudda told them that they were in the palace of the governor of Kufa, Ibn Ziyad. Yazid, who was the so-called caliph lived in Shaam and would send governors who would rule other cities under the kingdom on his behalf.

It was only a few days after the tragic day of Ashura and the women of the Ahlul Bayt and the fourth Imam had been imprisoned and brought to Ibn Ziyad's palace in Kufa and from there, were taken to Shaam. The children saw the family of Ahlul Bayt in shackles, chained, looking tired, bruised, hungry and thirsty. You could also see the pain of what had happened on the plains of Kerbala in their eyes.

Mrs. Hudda pointed to a particular corner of the court where the children saw Imam Zain al-Abideen (AS) who looked very ill. He had heavy chains around his hands and feet that made it very difficult to walk. He also had something around his neck that was making him bleed a lot.

Mrs. Hudda explained what that was. "Around Imam Zain al-Abideen (AS)'s neck is a kind of collar that has nails sticking out into his neck."

The children were in tears at the state of the Imam and the pain and suffering he was undergoing. They then noticed the women of the Imam's family all tied together by a single rope. Their hijaab had been snatched away and their hands had been tied to their necks.

"Aren't these guys Muslims? Why are they doing this to the family of their own Prophet?!" exclaimed Taha angrily.

"When you commit a sin, Taha, your heart tells you that it is wrong. But with every sin you commit, there is a black spot in your heart. And when you continue sinning, the mark gets bigger until your whole heart is covered with it! At that point your heart stops telling you that what you are doing is wrong. This is what has happened to these men. These oppressors' hearts have become so hard that nothing moves them anymore," she continued. "They have been blinded so much by greed and their sins that they don't even see the plight of the thirsty and tired orphans of the Holy Prophet Muhammed's family."

"But Mrs. Hudda, doesn't every action of a person have a reason? Why are they doing all this though?" Aliya asked innocently.

"Imam Hussain (AS) had refused to give allegiance to Yazid because he knew that Yazid was a very evil person. Because of that, Yazid had Imam Hussain (AS) killed. Now he and his people are trying to announce their so-called victory by parading the Ahlul Bayt as captives of the rebels that were killed in Kerbala. However, we see in history that their plans fail because of the heart-moving sermons of Imam Zain al-Abideen (AS), Lady Zainab (AS), and the other ladies in the courts and marketplaces of Kufa and Shaam. They spread the message of Kerbala to all the cities they were taken to and made the people realize the evil Yazid and his men had committed against the family of the Holy Prophet (SAW)."

Mrs. Hudda and all the children became silent when they heard the Imam begin his sermon in Kufa.

"O people! Whoever recognizes me knows me, and whoever does not, let me tell him that I am Ali son of al-Hussain son of Ali son of Abu Talib.

I am the son of the man whose holiness has been violated, whose wealth has been plundered, whose children have been seized.

I am the son of the one who has been slaughtered by the Euphrates, neither out of blood revenge nor on account of an inheritance.

I am the son of the one killed in the worst manner.

O people! I plead to you in the Name of Allah. Do you not know that you wrote to my father, and then deceived him?

Did you not grant him your word, your promise, and your allegiance, and then you fought him?

May you be ruined for what you have committed against your own souls, and out of your corrupt views!

Through what eyes will you look at the Messenger of Allah when he says to you, 'You killed my family, and violated my sanctity, so you do not belong to my nation?'

Although he was ill, imprisoned, and oppressed, there was an inner strength in him that was so evident. He had special strength and power given to him by Allah SWT who had chosen him as an Imam and the leader of all the believers. Even after having suffered so much at the hands of the oppressors, he continued to stand up for the truth. The children were filled with sadness at the state of the Ahlul Bayt, angry at the enemies, and filled with admiration for Imam Zain al-Abideen (AS). Through the sermon, they saw how Imam

Zain al-Abideen (AS) had made sure the truth was told. They learned how important it was to stand up for the truth no matter what condition you were in.

Suddenly, the children saw the Saheefa as-Sajjadiyya glowing. They gathered around the book, placed their hands on it and were taken forward in time to see the life of the Imam after he left Shaam.

"Where are we now?" Summayya asked. "I see a groom," shared Hadi. "And I see a bride... it must be a wedding!" exclaimed Sayyada.

The kids found themselves in a hall that was very well-decorated. Mrs. Hudda told them that the place was decorated for a wedding. A Shia follower of the Ahlul Bayt was having a majlis for Imam Hussain (AS) before his child's wedding.

Sabira pointed towards a man sitting at the entrance, where everyone had kept their shoes "Why is Imam Zain al-Abideen (AS) sitting over there?"

Just as the children turned to look, a man approached the Imam. He asked Imam Zain al-Abideen (AS), "Oh son of the Prophet! Why are you sitting over here?" Imam Zain al-Abideen responded, "My grandmother is here with me. I have come here because the host is remembering the oppression committed against my father, even on this happy occasion."

Mrs. Hudda told the children that after the event of Kerbala, Imam Zain al-Abideen's life had changed forever. He always encouraged the people to remember the martyrs of Kerbala who had sacrificed their lives for the truth and for the love of Allah SWT.

"Especially before drinking water," interjected Yasir. "Wait a minute! Did the Imam Zain al-

Abideen just say that his grandmother is also there?" asked Jawaad looking around.

A beautiful scent, like the scent of sweet roses, took the children by surprise. They noticed Lady Fatema (AS), sitting next to her grandson, listening to the majlis of Imam Hussain (AS).

Mrs. Hudda saw the amazement in the children's eyes and went on to explain that whenever there is a gathering to remember the martyrs of Kerbala, Lady Fatema (AS) visits the gathering. She will also intercede on their behalf of the Day of Judgment and seek forgiveness for their shortcomings.

Just then, the Saheefa as-Sajjadiyya began to glow again. With a blinding flash the children were taken to a dark room where they could hear someone crying softly as he whispered something in Arabic.

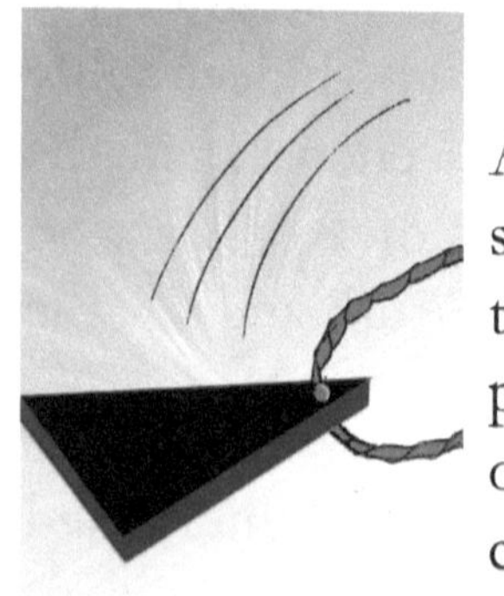

The triangular piece in Ammar's pocket began to shine. The children realized that it is the fourth Imam praying to Allah SWT. Like all other Imams, he had a very close and special relationship with Allah SWT.

When the entire world was fast asleep, Imam Zain al-Abideen (AS) would stay up to talk to his Master. Mrs. Hudda told them that the fourth Imam was known for his prayers and worship. Some of his titles like Sayyid as-Saajideen – master of those who do sujood, and Zain al-Abideen – the ornament of the worshippers, reflect his devotion to Allah SWT and prayers.

Ammar put his hand in his pocket and pulled out the silver piece that said 'Du'a' on it. He wore it around his neck and prayed to Allah SWT to strengthen his faith, so that he too could have a bond with the Almighty like Imam Sajjad (AS) did.

Shabbir noticed something. "Look at those two boys listening to Imam Sajjad. What are they doing? Are they writing down what he is reciting?"

"They are the Imam's sons: Imam Muhammed Baqir (AS) and Zayd," explained Mrs. Hudda. "The Imam's sons are writing down the du'as that the Imam is reciting. The du'as were then compiled into the…"

All the children started smiling and looked at the royal blue book with gold writing. Was this the book Mrs. Hudda was talking about? Together, with excitement, they exclaimed:

"That is exactly right! The book has du'as for everything ranging from when you are sick to when you are in fear to when you are in some difficulty."

"There are also du'as for every day of the week, prayers for parents, neighbors, among so many other things!" Ammar added. "You are very right Ammar," said Mrs. Hudda, looking at her watch.

"It is almost time to get back to the classroom" Mrs. Hudda told the class. They noticed the Saheefa shining and put their hands on the book. As they said "LABAYK YA IMAM," they were all zapped back into the classroom.

They formed their halaqa and started to discuss what they had learnt. The children took out their notebooks and started writing down the facts about the Imam that Mrs. Hudda had on the board.

Name: Ali

Birth Date: 5th of Shaban 38 A.H.

Father: Imam Hussain (AS)

Mother: Shahrbanu, an Iranian Princess

Died: 25th of Muharram 95 AH

Children: Imam Muhammed Baqir and others

Titles: Sayyid as-Saajideen (Master of all those who do sujood) and Zain al-Abideen (The Ornament of the Worshipers)

Buried: in Janatul Baqi, Medina,

Book he left for us: Sahifa as-Sajjadiyah

"Our fourth Imam taught us how to be patient through hard times, and always pray to the Almighty by whispering our secrets to Him and through du'a," Mrs. Hudda informed the class.

As the children went back to their desks to pack up for the day, they noticed a copy of Saheefa as-Sajjadiyya on their desks, with a note from Mrs. Hudda:

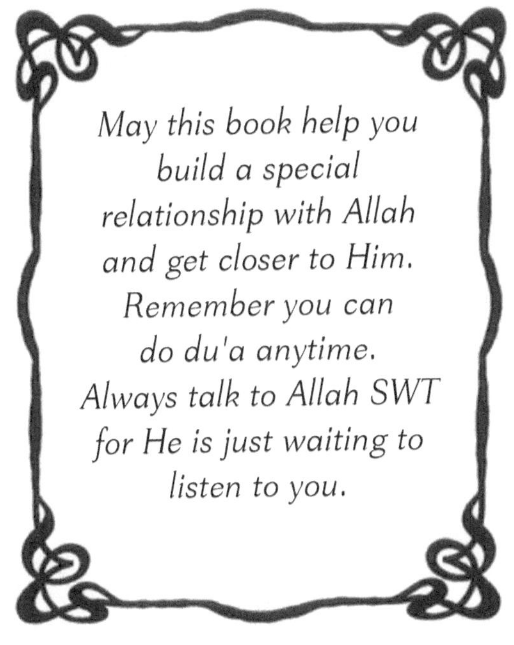

The children clustered around Mrs. Hudda to give her a hug and thank her for the wonderful present. From then on, each of them made a point to gather their entire family everyday and recite a du'a from the Saheefa as-Sajjadiyya. Some would do it before dinner and some would do it after. Others did it before or after the evening prayers.

Each student also made time during the day to work on building their relationship with Allah SWT by talking to Him, telling Him what they were happy or sad about, asking Him for help whenever they were in difficulty, and thanking Him for all His wonderful blessings. Mrs. Hudda made them realize that it's important to seek Allah in the GOOD times as well as the bad.

Each time Ammar sat on his prayer mat and did du'a, the shiny piece that had fallen out of the Saheefa would shine and glow.

Use this page to jot down anything you learned and that you think you can apply to your life.

Knowledge
& Humility
Imam Muhammed
al-Baqir (A.S)

RiNG! RiNG! RiNG!

Mrs. Hudda rubbed her eyes and stretched her arms and ran to grab the phone. Her eyes met her alarm clock - "6:00 am," she mumbled. "Who in the world would be calling me this early?"

"Mrs. Hudda, Salamun Alayki, it is Mr. Hashim here," said an anxious voice on the other end. Without even stopping for a breath, he continued, "I need a favor from you. Mr. Rahman has got chickenpox and won't be able to teach today. Would you be able to come in a bit early and teach Class 786? I know you may not have any material since it is last minute but you can have a free period. I just need someone in that classroom. Please? You are my only hope!"

"Mr. Hashim, always have hope in Allah SWT only. InshAllah, I'll be there soon!" she replied. She heard a sigh of relief from the other end. She quickly got dressed and left for Al-Iman Madrassah.

As she walked into the classroom, all the students were delighted to see her.

"Salaamun Alaykum. I am not sure if you have found out yet but Mr. Rahman is under the weather today. So I will be taking his class. I think you all have earned some free time! Please do remember that you are in Madrassah and you have to be respectful," Mrs. Hudda said.

All the students were ecstatic! Ammar, Yasir, Sibtain and Taha grabbed the Islamic board games and started playing. Fizza and Zainab went to the crafts station and started making a necklace for Mrs. Hudda. Talib, Shabbir, Imran and Sayyada rushed to the computer. Aunali went over to the bookshelf and grabbed a couple of books. He sat down on the soft, squishy bean bag and began to read.

"Pssst…look at that nerd reading over there. It's supposed to be free time!" snickered Shabbir.

Although Aunali could hear his classmates teasing him, he did not get discouraged. He found something really interesting in one of the books he had picked up and walked over to Mrs. Hudda to share it with her. The two started discussing the book.

"Yea…I know! Look, he is trying to impress Mrs. Hudda when it is free time. He is just a nerd!" teased Sayyada.

"Totally! I hate to read…books are so boring!" added Talib.

In the other corner of the classroom, Asiya was playing pretend with Aliya and Sabira. She stood in front of the chalk board pretending to be the two girls' teacher. When the girls couldn't answer the questions, Asiya got really frustrated. "I can't believe you don't know the answer to the question," Asiya said dramatically, upsetting the two girls. "Oh why oh why, do I have such dumb students!"

Mrs. Hudda observed everything that was going on as she prepared for the next class. On the writing easel next to the halaqa rug, she began to write:

1. The good of this world and the world to come is with knowledge.

2. The one who strives to seek knowledge, Allah (SWT) treads a way for that person to Jannah.

3. The angels spread their wings under the feet of those who seek knowledge.

4. All the angels and Allah (SWT)'s creations, even the fish swimming in the oceans, seek forgiveness for one who goes to seek knowledge.

As usual, Mrs. Hudda had a unique way of drawing her students' attention. When she turned around, she noticed more than half the class sitting on the halaqa rug, eagerly waiting for her to start the class.

Shabbir, Sayyada, Talib, and Asiya were the last ones to join her.

"Angels spread their wings under the one who is heading to acquire knowledge," Fizza read out loud. "No way!" she exclaimed.

"Even the fish ask for forgiveness for someone who is learning. Boy, I wish I hadn't wasted all that time sleeping in the classroom," Taha said in a disappointed tone.

Mrs. Hudda smiled gently at the kids. "I guess since everyone is here, we should just go ahead and start class early. Now who thinks they know what we are going to talk about today?" she questioned the anxious kids. Looking at the board, Aunali raised his hand and said "knowledge".

"What a know-it-all!" Shabbir muttered as he rolled his eyes.

"No, Mrs. Hudda. It's seeking knowledge. Aunali was wrong - he needs to be more specific next time," Asiya added, a little arrogantly.

"You are both right. Today we are going to talk about the importance of knowledge and seeking knowledge. Does anyone know of a man who is known as the Treasurer of Knowledge? The man who taught over 300 scholars," she continued.

The children noticed the mysterious twinkle in Mrs. Hudda's eyes as they tried to guess the answer. She walked over to the bookshelf and pulled out a small golden coin from between the books on the shelf.

"Baqir al-Uloom" she told the kids "The Treasurer of Knowledge."

"That is our fifth Imam, Imam Muhammed al-Baqir (AS)," Yasir exclaimed.

Mrs. Hudda nodded in approval as she brought the golden coin to the halaqa rug. She placed the coin in the center of the rug and whispered "LABAYK YA IMAM."

Just like before something fell out, but this time it was two clay triangular pieces that rolled out from where the coin lay on the rug. The kids watched in astonishment as one piece came to stop where Asiya sat. She picked it up with trembling hands and saw "Humility" engraved on it. The other piece rolled across the circle and stopped at Shabbir. He picked it up and read the word 'Knowledge'. Both of them put it in their pockets.

The kids, realizing that this time they would go back to the past without even touching the coin, repeated after Mrs. Hudda

"LABAYK YA IMAM"

In a matter of seconds, they were transported back to the time of Imam Muhammed Baqir (AS). They found themselves in a room where the Imam used to teach his companions and students. Mrs. Hudda could see the delight on the children's faces as they stared at the bright, luminous face of Imam Baqir (AS). He had an aura of perfection, piety, and humbleness in him; they could not take their eyes off him.

One of the students of the Imam approached him with a question:

"O son of the Prophet, has Allah given human beings free will so that they can do whatever they want or is our life already determined by fate?" Imam Baqir (AS) asked the student to raise one of his feet in mid-air. The student did as he was told. The Imam then asked him to raise both his feet. The student protested, "Ya Imam, I'll fall if I do that."

Imam Muhammed Baqir (AS) then explained that similarly, Allah SWT has given us the power of will to make decisions but has placed restrictions on that power. The children had awe in their faces. The Imam could answer deep, philosophical questions in such a practical way.

Realizing what the children were thinking about, Mrs. Hudda started to explain further. "The Imam had a unique way of explaining the most complex phenomenon. Whenever Imam Muhammed Baqir (AS) taught, he shed the drops of knowledge and wisdom upon the hearts of his students like a saturated cloud. Everyone benefited, each person would understand the concept according to his or her own level of understanding."

The setting around them then began to change. A few seconds later, the children realized that they were in Imam Muhammed Baqir (AS)'s home. They looked around Imam's house, and admired the simplicity with which the Imam lived.

"Knock! Knock! Knock!" There was someone at the door. When Imam Baqir (AS) answered the door, the children found out that it was the messenger of Abdul Malik ibn Marwan (the ruler of the Muslim Empire). "The King needs your help at this instance," came the request.

The children hurriedly followed Imam Muhammed Baqir (AS) to Abdul Malik's palace. A man stopped the Imam and started mocking the Imam, calling him "Baqr".

"What's Baqr?" Aliya asked Mrs. Hudda.

"Baqr means cow," replied Mrs. Hudda. "In an attempt to make fun of the Imam, the man called him Baqr instead of calling him Baqir, which means the one who splits knowledge."

"I feel like pouncing on him!" Jawaad exclaimed in anger. The triangular piece around his neck that said 'Peace and Anger Management' reminded him to calm down.

Imam Muhammed Baqir (AS) calmly and politely told the man, "No, I am not Baqr, I am Baqir.

The man continued his insults: "You are the son of the woman who was a cook."

"That was her career," responded Imam Muhammed Baqir (AS) calmly. "There is nothing shameful in it."

The man continued to mock the Imam and accused his mother of being a bad person.

"If the matters you accuse my mother of are true, I ask Allah SWT to forgive her sins. And if they are false, I ask Allah SWT to forgive you for your accusations and lies," replied Imam Baqir (AS).

"That's another example of someone who treats those who are mean to him with kindness," said Talib.

Mrs. Hudda nodded. "One of the signs of wisdom is that a person develops an inner calmness. People's actions no longer affect a person that has that inner calmness because they are just like stones thrown into a vast ocean – they only create ripples on the surface but can't affect the calmness in the depth of that ocean. In other words, knowledge brings a person to another level. It makes them think about their words and actions before they say or do anything."

Shabbir started thinking about what he had said about Aunali being a nerd. Asiya also felt guilty about her rude remarks to her friends. They both learnt a lesson from the Imam who was The Treasurer of Knowledge, but was still very humble and kind to his friends as well as those who hated him.

The children continued to follow Imam Baqir (AS) until they reached Abdul Malik's palace.

As soon as he noticed the Imam, Abdul Malik desperately narrated the dilemma that he, as the ruler of the Muslim empire, faced. The Christians in Egypt, which was a Muslim country, had started making paper money with a Christian logo of father-son-holy spirit.

When Abdul Malik ordered the Egyptians to stop printing money with the Christian logo, the Caesar of Rome threatened to print abusive language about the Holy Prophet (SAW) on the Roman coins. This had really put Abdul Malik in a dangerous position because the Muslim Empire was using the Roman currency and the Roman coins. None of his advisors could help him in this desperate situation. Thus, he had turned to the grandson of the Holy Prophet (SAW) and the Treasurer of Knowledge to help him.

Mrs. Hudda explained that the Caliphs who stole the rights of the Ahlul Bayt and oppressed them always turned to the Imam of the time when Islam was in danger – because they knew that they were the rightful leaders Allah SWT had appointed for the Muslims. And as usual, when Islam was at stake, the Imam of the time helped the same ruler that unjustly took his rights in order to save Islam.

Imam Muhammed Baqir (AS) told Abdul Malik that the Muslim Empire should start making its own coins, with "La ilaha ilallah" on one side and "Muhammedun Rasulullah" on the other. If they had their own coins, the Muslims would not need to use the Roman coins. If no Muslim used Roman coins, it would be pointless for the Caesar to print insulting words against the Holy Prophet (SAW) on the Roman coins.

Asiya admired the nature of the Imam. Even with his enemies, he was not boastful about being the one to find the solution to such a big problem. She regretted her comments to Aliya and Sabira, as well as her condescending comment about Aunali's answer.

The coin started to glow and the children realized it was time to head back to class. They chanted "LABAYK YA IMAM, LABAYK YA IMAM," and were zapped back into their classroom.

The excited children formed their halaqa with their notebooks and pencils ready in their hands, and each one of them shared what they had learnt from Imam Muhammed Baqir (AS).

Turning to Aunali, Shabbir apologized, "Aunali, I am very sorry for teasing you like that. Now, I know how important seeking knowledge is."

"That's okay, bro! Don't worry about it." replied Aunali. Asiya, encouraged by Shabbir's apology, turned to her friends too.

"Yeah Aliya and Sabira, I am also sorry for being so arrogant. I don't know everything and shouldn't act like a Miss Know-it-all! I promise I am going to try not to be arrogant anymore."

Aliya and Sabira were astonished at the change the Imam's actions brought to their big-headed friend. They realized that Allah SWT's guidance can really change a person. They were speechless and all they could do was give Asiya a warm hug and were friends again.

"I really admired how Imam Muhammed Baqir (AS) used such practical examples to explain very complex things," Imran mentioned.

"Also how he was so calm regardless of the situation he was in," added Jawaad.

"And can you believe that the Imam was willing to help the Caliph as well? He had just the perfect answer that solved all the problems. His solution set standards for all the transactions in the Muslim world," Fizza said with a beaming smile. Each student added their two-cents as they went around the halaqa. At the very end, a reformed Shabbir tied the triangular piece with the word 'Knowledge' engraved on it around his neck and added to the class discussion. "Now I know why the hadith says even the fish swimming in the oceans seek forgiveness for the person who sets off to seek knowledge. I have learnt to appreciate our school, classes and our teachers for instilling the love for knowledge in our hearts."

Mrs. Hudda's heart was at rest as she listened to what each child had learnt from the Imam. The class had come a very long way in just seven weeks. As she started writing some information about the Imam on the chalk board, she thanked Allah SWT for helping her bring out the brighter side of these students.

Name: Muhammed

Title: Baqir-ul-uloom (The
        Treasurer of Knowledge)

Birthday: 1st Rajab, 57 AH

Father: Imam Zain-ul-Abideen

Mother: Fatimah Bint al-Hassan
(daughter of the 2nd Imam)

Died: 7th Dhul hijjah, 116 AH at
the age of 57

Cause of Death: poisoned by
Hisham ibn Abdul Malik

Buried in Jannatul Baqi, Medina

When the bell rang signaling the end of class, everyone rushed out of the class except Asiya. She sat on the halaqa rug staring at her triangular piece. Mrs. Hudda joined her on the rug and smiled at her when she looked up.

"Anytime we talk about a Masumeen or learn about their life, we always learn something that we need to take home with us and apply in our daily lives. Through these lessons, the Imam continues to guide us every single day of our lives," Mrs. Hudda told Asiya. "You have learnt a very important lesson today that I know you will take home with you."

Asiya nodded, with tears in her eyes. She asked Mrs. Hudda to help her hook the triangular piece to her bracelet so that it would constantly remind her of the lesson she had learnt from the fifth Imam, Imam Muhammed Baqir (AS). Mrs. Hudda smiled as she watched the changed Asiya walk out of the classroom.

Use this page to jot down anything you learned and that you think you can apply to your life.

Intelligence
Imam Jafar as-Ṣaqiq (A.S)

It was minutes before class started and Sumayya was sharing her grievances with Sabira. "I really love Mrs. Hudda, but I just wish I didn't have to come to Madrassah today. I have a huge Science test on Monday that I haven't even studied for," Sumayya sadly murmured.

"Well, you know my mom says Madrassah is just as important as school," Sabira said, hoping to cheer up her friend.

"Yeah…I know it's important but it's not a big deal if you fail in Madrassah. I can't afford to fail the semester exam at school, you know? I would be in BIG trouble… And plus you don't really NEED the kind of stuff we learn in Madrassah to be a doctor or a nurse. I guess I have to focus more on school," replied Sumayya.

Amir interrupted the two girls talking, "You know what my dad says? He says Islam is a way of life! Being a good Muslim means you are well-rounded in life."

"What is that supposed to mean?" asked Sumayya.

"What I mean is that you have the best of everything. Islam is not only your religion, but your way of life, so you apply it everywhere, even in your education. Remember when we went to visit the 5th Imam, Imam Muhammed al-Baqir (AS), we learnt that Islam values knowledge so much," clarified Amir.

Mrs. Hudda headed towards the girls and Amir. Their conversation seemed to have caught her attention as she walked in the classroom. "You know, Sumayya, when you go off to college and university, you will be learning a lot of things that were first taught by our Imams."

"Really? Mrs. Hudda sometimes I think you just make things up," Sumayya said sarcastically.

Mrs. Hudda smiled at Sumayya's comment. "I am not kidding. Let's see, who wants to be an astronaut?" All the boys and Sayyada yelled at the top of their lungs "ME!" hoping Mrs. Hudda would use a Space book and zap them into Space.

To their disappointment, they weren't zapped anywhere. Mrs. Hudda continued, "Well when you go to university, you will be learning about a great person by the name of Geber. Geber made a lot of contributions to Astronomy, Maths, and other Sciences. His real name was Jabir bin Hayyan. He was a student of the sixth Imam, Imam Jafar as-Sadiq (AS) and all the contributions he has made to modern science are what he learnt from OUR sixth IMAM." The children looked puzzled, but interested.

"Yes, you heard correctly. To be honest with you, if you want to become a doctor or an accountant or anything else, you should know that our Imams have contributed in those areas as well."

"Mrs. Hudda, how do you know all this?" asked Shabbir.

"Iqra! Read! It was the first word that was revealed to the Holy Prophet (SAW). Read! READ! Read! And I'm telling you to do the same," encouraged Mrs. Hudda.

"Now, who can tell me what they know about our sixth Imam?" asked Mrs. Hudda

Fizza's hand shot up in the air. "His name is Jafar and he's the son of the fifth Imam, Imam Muhammed Baqir (AS)."

"Excellent!" said Mrs. Hudda. "Anybody else?"

Amir spoke from the other side of the classroom, "He is often called Jafar as-Sadiq. That's his title, the Truthful One."

"And he has the same birthday as our Holy Prophet (SAW), which is the 17th of Rabbi-ul-Awwal," said Aunali confidently.

"You children seem to have done your research. Those are all very important facts about him. Does anyone know his mother's name?" asked Mrs. Hudda.

She looked at the blank faces staring at her and smiled. "Her name was Umm Farwah."

Mrs. Hudda walked over to the bookshelf and pulled out a Physics book with a picture of an astronaut dressed in white, floating in mid-air on the moon.

As she stood with the book in her hands, she explained how life was at the time of the sixth Imam. "The Caliphs from the time of the second Imam were from the Ummayyad family. At the time of the sixth Imam, another family, called the Abbassid family, was trying to take over the kingdom.

There was a lot of fighting between the two families and they were so busy that they weren't paying attention to the Imam of the time. The Imam of the time was our sixth Imam, Imam Jafar as-Sadiq. Because he was free to practice and preach Islam, he made full use of the time to share as much knowledge as he could."

"Wow! That is so cool," said Amir.

"Imam Jafar as-Sadiq (AS) used the time he had to teach the people about Islam. He also opened up one of the first universities where he taught all kinds of subjects. He taught Astronomy, Medicine, Maths, and so much more. It is said that he had up to 4,000 students."

"4,000?" echoed Sumayya, looking shocked.

"Yes, and Geber, or Jabir, was one of them. Don't you want to know more about this great person who is our Imam?" Mrs. Hudda saw the curiosity in the children's eyes, and they noticed that mysterious twinkle in hers. Not waiting a second, they all jumped out of their chairs, ran towards her and put their hands on the book.

"LABAYK YA IMAM"

...they said eagerly, as Sumayya picked up the triangular piece with 'Intellect' engraved on it and put it in her pocket.

With the blink of an eye, they were zapped into the past. The children found themselves cramped behind a red, velvety curtain in a huge palace. They were excited as they watched with curiosity, a king distributing wealth from the state's treasury.

"This is Mansur, the second Caliph or ruler from the Abbasid family," Mrs. Hudda whispered.

The children saw a man who seemed a little frustrated trying to get something from the treasury, but he didn't seem to be very successful.

"That man over there is Shakrani. His grandfather was a slave freed by the Holy Prophet (SAW) and because of that, a lot of people look up to him. The thing is, he does a lot of things that he shouldn't be doing. Like right now, he's trying to get his hands on something from the treasury," Mrs. Hudda explained.

Shakrani saw Imam Jafar as-Sadiq (AS) and the students also saw him. They didn't need to ask who that man was, as his features were very similar to the other Masumeen they had seen, and his face was glowing. His eloquence and splendor filled the room.

Shakrani turned desperately to Imam Jafar as-Sadiq (AS) and said, "Oh Imam, do you think YOU could help me get something from the king?"

The children watched as Imam Jafar as- Sadiq (AS) walked over to the king and brought something back for Shakrani.

As he handed it to Shakrani, Imam Jafar as-Sadiq (AS)said, "A good deed is good from everyone but it is better to occur from you, one who is associated with us. And a bad deed is bad from everyone, but it is worse from you, one who is associated with us." The Imam then walked off, leaving Shakrani in deep thought. Mrs. Hudda and the class walked out of the palace quietly.

"What do you think Imam Jafar as-Sadiq (AS) meant by what he said to Shakrani?" said Sumayya, puzzled.

Imran, after thinking for a moment, said "I think he meant that good deeds are good and bad deeds are bad, BUT each of them weighs heavier in their goodness and badness when done by someone who loves the Ahlul Bayt."

"Like for example, if we do something forbidden, like listen to music, it is worse than if someone who doesn't love the Imam did it?" asked Fizza.

"Yup! Well, that's what I think," Imran replied.

Confused, Sayyada questioned it further. "But I don't get it, why?"

It seemed like everyone was curious, and Taha decided to say what he thought all this meant. "I guess because you're supposed to know better. The Imams have struggled so much to teach us all our principles and values. It is worse if we say we love them but we don't follow their teachings, right?"

"That seems to make a lot of sense. Now I understand. Thanks guys." Sayyada was content with the answers and it seemed that Mrs. Hudda was also content. As she watched and heard her students discuss the matter further, she truly felt that they were no longer children but young adults, who were learning to use logic and common sense to put the pieces of the puzzle together and understand the Masumeen and their teachings.

The children began walking to the heart of the city, when all of a sudden, they heard curious whispers and stopped to listen. They heard a man in the crowd whisper to another, "Abu Hanifa is giving a talk today, let's see what he has to say."

Curiosity got the better of the children and Mrs. Hudda, and they decided to stay and listen to what Abu Hanifa had to say. Who was Abu Hanifa, the children wondered. They were about to find out.

Abu Hanifa walked to the center of the crowd and with a loud voice he began. "Although I have a great deal of respect for the grandson of the Holy Prophet (SAW), Jafar as-Sadiq, as I have been his student myself, I disagree with him on three things.

Firstly, I do not understand how Allah can exist but cannot be seen by anyone in this world or in the hereafter.

Secondly, the grandson of the Holy Prophet (SAW) says that Shaitan will be thrown into the hellfire. How can the hell fire hurt Shaitan who himself is made of fire?

And lastly, how is it in Allah's justice that He punishes and rewards people for their deeds when they don't have any control over their actions and He controls everything?"

The crowd looked confused and puzzled. Who was going to answer these questions? Aliya started to cringe. Though she wasn't too eager to admit it, she thought that Abu Hanifa was asking good questions.

For a minute or two, there was total silence. Abu Hanifa demanded an answer.

A young man silently walked to the middle of the crowd where Abu Hanifa stood, and picked up some clay.

With no warning whatsoever, the young man threw the clay at him. Abu Hanifa first looked startled at being struck, and then became angry. He cried out in pain and his men ran to get a hold of the man who threw the clay.

"Who is that man and what did he do that for?" Yasir was shocked.

Mrs. Hudda explained, "That is Bahlool, a very close companion and student of Imam Jafar as-Sadiq (AS)."

"What's going to happen now?" Amir just couldn't wait.

"Watch, and learn from the words of Bahlool," responded Mrs. Hudda calmly.

Abu Hanifa angrily spoke to the young man."What do you think you are doing? Do you know how much you hurt me with that clay?"

"Hurt you?" said Bahlool, "that is ridiculous! I don't see any pain. How can you prove that the pain is there, if I can't see it and nobody else can see it?"

"It is there!" said Abu Hanifa with frustration.

"In the same way, Allah SWT is there. Just because you can't see Him, does not mean He is not there. A true believer can feel Him, just like you felt the pain.

To answer your second question, how can Shaitan burn in the hell fire if he is made of fire and so is the hell fire? Well, you are made of clay aren't you? So if clay can hurt clay, then by Allah SWT's infinite wisdom, fire can also burn fire."

People in the crowd were shocked and moved by Bahlool's responses.

Aliya could not believe it! A man so confident was providing answers to questions that were so challenging.

"You must be punished for hurting me," said Abu Hanifa in anger. "Take him away!"

"How can you punish me? You said Allah SWT has control over all things, so He made me do it. You can't punish me," Bahlool responded.

Abu Hanifa was speechless and embarrassed as Bahlool provided excellent answers to all three of his questions. Abu Hanifa thought he would be smart, but instead Bahlool showed he was smarter!

The children giggled and laughed. The crowd slowly separated, talking in excitement about the event that had just taken place. It was time for the children to also move on, and they began to walk away.

The class walked and walked until they reached a place that was mostly deserted, with the exception of a few people. They saw three pillars in the middle of the deserted plains. Amir began to think that this place looked so familiar. "This is Mina!! Isn't it? It looks just like the pictures I have at home."

"Yes, it is," Mrs. Hudda replied with a smile.

"What is here? Why have we come here?" Yasir asked with a puzzled look. "Isn't that Imam Jafar as-Sadiq (AS), over there?" Sumayya said, pointing in the distance.

"Yeah! There's the Imam!" The children began to talk all at once. They walked closer so that they could see Imam Jafar as- Sadiq (AS).

Imam Jafar as-Sadiq (AS) was with some companions buying some grapes. A man, who looked poor and tired, approached the sixth Imam and asked him for something to eat. The Imam handed him a bunch of grapes.

The poor man frowned and the children leaned in to hear properly as he muttered, "I want money, not grapes."

"May Allah SWT provide you that," came Imam Jafar Sadiq (AS)'s gentle reply.

Another man, who also looked poor and tired, walked up to the Imam and asked for help too. Imam Jafar as-Sadiq (AS) gave him a bunch of grapes.

The poor man said "Alhamdulillah," As he took them. The sixth Imam then gave him another handful of grapes. The poor man again said "Alhamdulillah". Imam Jafar as-Sadiq (AS) then gave him 20 dirhams.

The poor man looked up to the skies and said "Alhamdulillah".

Imam Jafar as-Sadiq (AS) then took off the cloak he was wearing and gave that to the beggar too.

The poor man then looked at Imam, said "Thank you my Imam," and walked away.

The children were confused as to what had just happened. The people who also saw this happen asked Imam Jafar as-Sadiq (AS) why did he give so much to one beggar and little to the other. Imam Jafar Sadiq (AS) explained, "The second poor man kept thanking Allah SWT, so I kept on giving, for it was His command." The children were very impressed by the Imam's generosity and wisdom.

"Why did Imam Jafar as-Sadiq (AS) act so differently between the two beggars?" asked Mrs. Hudda, wanting to ensure the children understood the importance of thanking Allah SWT.

"Was it because the second beggar kept thanking Allah SWT, and was thankful for whatever he was given?" Amir asked, thoughtfully.

"The first beggar seemed a little arrogant, he wasn't satisfied with what he was given," added Talib.

"That kind of reminds me of the saying: 'Beggars can't be choosers'," said Sakina.

"No matter where you get something from, you should always keep in mind that the person giving you is just a way of getting it to you. It's all from Allah SWT, so you should always thank Allah

SWT in addition to thanking the person who gives you something."

"We should understand that Allah SWT knows in His ultimate wisdom what is best for us, and what we are in need of," reminded Mrs. Hudda.

"So true," said Sabira.

"I think our time is almost up. What do you guys think about going back to class before someone notices that we're gone?" said Mrs. Hudda, a bit reluctantly.

"Time just seems to fly when we are with you on one of these adventures, Mrs. Hudda," said Amir.

The children gathered around and placed their hands on the book. You could hear the sounds of "LABAYK YA IMAM" throughout the city as the children were zapped back into their classroom.

The children raced to the halaqa rug and began their discussion. Each child had realized that the Masumeen are our role models and that they needed to learn the valuable lessons from the stories they saw and read about, and use these lessons in their lives.

As usual, they all went around in a circle and, one by one, shared what they had learnt.

"Let's start with you, Amir," said Mrs. Hudda

"You should always thank Allah SWT when you get something nice."

"Being snotty doesn't get you anything!" said Sayyada, who was next in the circle

All the children chuckled at Sayyada's abrupt and blunt comment.

"Your actions should be good because that is what is expected of you as a follower of the Masumeen," said Shabbir.

Fizza continued, "A bad deed or a sin is worse when it comes from a follower of the Masumeen, because they should know better."

"Knowledge really comes in handy. I love how Bahlool proved Abu Hanifa wrong," contributed Yasir.

"I agree," said Aliya, "that was the coolest thing I saw."

Mrs. Hudda turned to Sumayya and asked her, "So what about your thoughts about the things you learn about in Madrassah."

"Islam is a way of life so the Masumeen came with Islamic knowledge as well as knowledge of all of Allah SWT's creation. So learning about that is also rewarding if you use it in the right way. I learnt how Imam Jafar as-Sadiq (AS) was an excellent teacher by listening to Bahlool, who was his student, and I also learnt how he didn't only teach Islam, but other subjects as well, because they all go together, hand in hand" said Sumayya.

"In other words, having both the secular school and religious education gives you a great deal of advantages in both this world and the hereafter. You should keep a good balance between the importance you give to School and Madrassah," responded Mrs. Hudda.

"I learned it so important to use our intellect. You know what they say, if you don't use it, you lose it! We have to use our brains every day, otherwise we will lose it." Shabbir added.

"Don't be lazy, let your mind go crazy learning! Remember the hadith, 'Seek knowledge from cradle to grave" Imran shared.

Mrs. Hudda's heart was beaming with pride. She looked at her students and knew that this bunch of kids was special. She whispered a little prayer to Allah SWT,

"Oh Allah increase my knowledge and the knowledge of my students. Ameen"

"Mrs. Hudda," Amir thoughtfully asked, "How was the sixth Imam martyred?"

"Mansur, the Abbasid Caliph, had Imam Jafar as-Sadiq poisoned in Medina on the 25th of Shawwal. He was then buried in Jannatul Baqi close to his his father, Imam Muhammed Baqir (AS), and our other Imams, Imam Hassan (AS), and Imam Zain al-Abideen (AS)."

Sumayya, with a mix of curiosity and anger, asked, "Why would he do something like that? Why would he poison the Imam?"

"Mansur was worried that if Imam Jafar Sadiq (AS) continued to spread knowledge the way he was doing, people would soon realize that the Imam is an appointed leader from Allah SWT and they would overthrow Mansur. Therefore, he had the Imam poisoned so he could continue to stay in power."

The children quickly copied the facts from the board as the bell was about to ring.

Name: Jafar

Title: As-Sadiq (The Truthful One)

Mother: Umm Farwah

Father: 5th Imam - Imam Muhammed Baqir (AS)

Children: Imam Musa al-Kadhim (and others)

Birthday: 17th Rabbi Awwal 83AH

Died on: 25th Shawwal 148AH

Buried: Jannatul Baqi, Medina

Interesting Facts: He made a lot of contributions to modern sciences, and taught us that Islam is not just a religion, but a way of life.

Sumayya tied the triangular piece that said 'Intellect' around her neck, as she prayed to the Almighty to help her be intelligent in Islam as well as in her goal to become a doctor, because she now understood that they were two pieces of the same puzzle.

"Ameen!" Mrs. Hudda whispered as the children walked out of the room.

Use this page to jot down anything you learned and that you think you can apply to your life.

Kindness
&
Patience
Imam Musa
al-Kadhim (A.S)

As Mrs. Hudda walked up the stairs to the classroom, she noticed Aliya sitting outside the door, sniffling and wiping tears from her eyes. Alarmed at the sight of the distraught girl, Mrs. Hudda asked, "What happened, Aliya?"

"Sabira is a snob!" sobbed Aliya. "She thinks she is better than everybody! She told me she was better than me in everything. I just rolled my eyes and told her I hate her and left!"

"Everything will be just fine," Mrs. Hudda reassured the little girl. "Let's go inside, class is about to begin. I will make sure I talk to her before class is over."

As the two of them walked into the classroom, Mrs. Hudda could sense the tension between Aliya and Sabira.

Unfortunately, she could also see some of the boys grinning, anticipating some drama between the two girls. Aliya quietly walked over to her desk giving Sabira a mean look as she passed her.

Mrs. Hudda saw that now all the students were paying attention to the two girls. She cleared her throat in an attempt to divert their attention to her. She gave them a warm smile and the twinkle in her eyes told them that the adventure they were going to experience would be much more interesting than the fight between the two girls.

All the children found a comfortable spot on the halaqa rug. Aliya and Sabira sat as far apart from each other as humanly possible. Having caught everyone's attention, Mrs. Hudda walked over to the bookshelf. On the bottom rack, there were prayer mats, clothes for prayer, turbas, tasbeehs, and other items the class used for Salaat. She slowly took out a prayer mat that looked very different from the other ones. It was glowing and very luminous. Mrs. Hudda brought it over to the halaqa rug and placed it in the center.

"Salaat was very important to all our Imams – after all, it is the foundation of our faith," she began. "Their dedication to it was unwavering regardless of the circumstances they were in. Worship of Allah SWT was their first priority whether they were in the middle of a major battle, in prison or anywhere else. In good times and in bad times, Allah SWT was always in their hearts…"

Everyone put their hands on the prayer mat and said,

'LABAYK YA IMAM'

A tiny triangular piece rolled out of the prayer mat with 'Kindness & Patience' engraved on it. Aliya eagerly grabbed the piece and read the special words.

She joined the rest of her classmates in saying "LABAYK YA IMAM". In a matter of seconds, the class was zapped back to the time of the seventh Imam, Imam Musa al-Kadhim (AS). They found themselves in the streets of Medina. They saw a group of men walking towards the mosque. Mrs. Hudda pointed out the seventh Imam, Imam Musa al-Kadhim (AS) to the class.

As the class observed Imam Musa al-Kadhim (AS)'s kind behavior with his companions, they noticed an old Arab man approaching the Imam. The Arab started insulting Imam Musa al-Kadhim (AS) and used foul language against him. Imam al-Kadhim's companions asked for the Imam's permission to answer back to the Arab's rude conduct. Instead of allowing them to teach the guy a lesson, Imam Musa al-Kadhim (AS) asked them to leave the man alone. Though they have seen the previous Imams act in a similar manner, the children stared at Imam Musa al-Kadhim's conduct in amazement.

"Wow…that must have taken a lot of inner strength to let the guy go," Aliya said with awe.

"The old me would definitely have let my friends beat the life out of him, but with all our adventures we are learning so much. Being good to those who are not good to you is an act that Allah SWT loves, and each of our Imams have taught us that!" Jawaad shared.

As the kids discussed the Imam's behavior, they noticed the day turning into night and the night turning into day again. Mrs. Hudda told the class that the next incident occurred a number of days after the incident they had just witnessed. They saw Imam al-Kadhim (AS) again at the same place, asking about the rude man that had been so horrible to him. A companion of the Imam responded, "He has moved away to the countryside to work on his farms."

Having heard that, the Imam got on his horse and started heading towards the countryside. The kids hopped on a carriage heading in the same direction and followed the Imam.

Upon seeing the Arab man working on the fields, the Imam got off his horse and headed towards the man. As before, the man started insulting the Imam. The Imam kindly asked the man, "How much have you spent on these fields?"

The man, surprised at Imam's interest in his livelihood, responded "a hundred dinaars."

The Imam continued to question him. "How much profit do you expect to make from them?"

"Two hundred dinaars," replied the man.

Imam Kadhim (AS) then took out a bag containing three hundred dinaar and handed it to the man. The man was astonished at Imam's generosity and kindness even though he had been so rude to him.

"Wow! The man learnt his lesson," Jawaad said thoughtfully, "and the Imam did not even have to lose his cool to teach him one."

"Have you guys noticed that all our Masumeen have always treated everyone kindly, regardless of how they have been treated by the person?" Yassir added.

Aliya thought back to how she had reacted in the class when Sabira was rude to her. "I guess it is one of the hardest things to do - show kindness to those who are mean to you."

"Hey guys!" Ammar said, grabbing everyone's attention. "Where is Imam Musa al-Kadhim (AS) going?" The class quickly rushed to keep up with the Imam. The kids followed the Imam back into the city where he met his companions. The children then noticed a poor man approaching the Imam and his companions.

Imam Musa al-Kadhim (AS) greeted the poor man cheerfully, "Asalaamun Alaykum, brother."

"Alaykum Salaam," the poor man answered the Imam.

The Imam went on to inquire about the poor man's family. After talking for a while, the Imam and the poor man bid farewell to each other.

One of the companions criticized the Imam for talking to a poor man, telling him that it was beneath him to talk to such a man. "What were you doing talking to that poor man? How can a man like you, a great Imam, talk to a poor ordinary man like that in public?!"

"Are we not equal in the eyes of Allah?" the Imam questioned his companion.

Embarrassed, the companion tried to justify himself, "Yes, oh Imam but…"

The Imam continued, "My friend, because a man is poor today does not mean he will be poor tomorrow. A man you help today may help you tomorrow. We are all equal."

After seeing that, it was time for Sabira to reflect over her actions. Ashamed about her arrogant attitude, she murmured, "We are all equal in the eyes of Allah regardless of whether we are rich or poor. Petty things like that don't make anyone better than somebody else."

"We can learn a lot from our Masumeen. They teach us many different lessons from the incidents in their lives," Mrs. Hudda explained. "Another lesson we can learn from him is patience. Like our other Imams, the seventh Imam also faced a lot of trials and difficulties."

"Mrs. Hudda, my daddy says that Allah tests those he loves most," Sayyada said.

"What kind of trials did Imam Musa al-Kadhim (AS) face?" Talib asked curiously.

"Let us gather around and go a few years forward to the time when Imam Musa al-Kadhim (AS) was put in prison," came the answer.

The prayer mat started glowing and the class was taken into a dark prison where they saw the Imam in sajdah.

The class could hear the Imam whispering munajaat to Allah SWT – praising and glorifying Him. To the children's amazement, instead of complaining to Allah SWT for being imprisoned without having committed any wrong and asking Him to free him from the prison, the Imam thanked Allah SWT for his imprisonment!

"Wow!" Aliya exclaimed. "That's such a different angle to look at things from!"

Saddened by the state of the Imam, Fizza asked, "But why was he put in prison if he had not done anything wrong? I am really getting tired of these rulers who imprison and hurt our Imams."

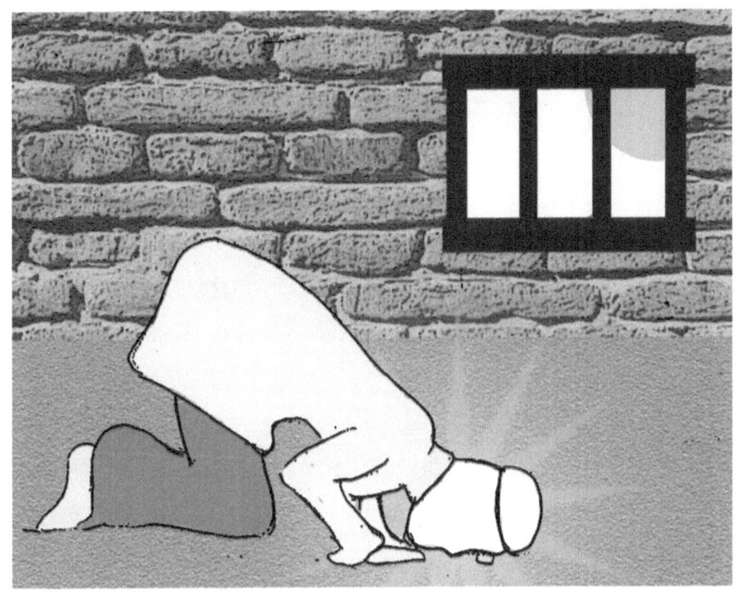

"Haroon Rashid was the Abbasid Caliph at the time of the seventh Imam," Mrs. Hudda started to explain. "And like every Imam, Imam Musa al-Kadhim had the kindness and leadership that people loved and cherished. The Caliphs also realized that the leadership really belonged to the grandsons of the Holy Prophet (SAW) and that they had unjustly stolen it. Because of that, the Caliphs were always afraid that a time would come when the Imam's followers would rebel against their oppression and injustice. So the Caliphs, like this one, thought that imprisoning the seventh Imam was the only way to keep him away from his followers and prevent a revolt."

"What about all his companions? Didn't they do something? I mean if I was there, I would start a revolt! It's okay to stand up for the truth and get mad when oppression is done on the innocent." Jawaad said in a frustrated tone.

"Haroon was a very evil ruler. He used oppression and hypocrisy to stay in power," Mrs. Hudda answered. "He would act like he was a very nice Muslim to stop the people of the nation from finding out the truth. When he couldn't cover his actions any more, he would commit so much oppression that people would be afraid of even speaking out against him." Mrs. Hudda went on to tell the kids, "Eventually, he had Imam Musa al-Kadhim (AS) poisoned and martyred."

All the children gasped. How could someone kill such a pious and humble man? What harm had the Imam ever done to Haroon? There was a moment of silence as the kids quietly thought about the sacrifices the Masumeen had given in order to save Islam.

"You know guys, regardless of the difficulties they had, all our Masumeen willingly sacrificed everything they had so that we would know what the true message of Islam is," Yasir told the class.

"Yeah!" Ammar added. "Had it not been for them, the Caliphs would have changed all the rules and principles of Islam to suit them and we would no longer know what the true message of Islam is!"

Suddenly, the class noticed the prayer mat glowing. Their surroundings started to fade slightly and they realized it was time to go back. They placed their hands on the prayer mat and softly said "LABAYK YA IMAM" twice. In a split second, they found themselves on the halaqa rug sitting around the prayer mat – just like they were before they were taken back to the past.

Mrs. Hudda started writing some basic information about the Imam on the class chalkboard. The kids eagerly grabbed their notebooks and started writing them down as well.

Name: Musa al-Kadhim (AS)

Title: al-Kadhim (The one who restrains his anger) and Baabul Hawaaij (The Door of Fulfillment of Wishes)

Father: Imam Jafar as-Sadiq

Mother: Hameeda

Children: Imam ar-Ridha and Lady Fatema Masuma

Birthday: 7th Safar, 128 AH

Born in: Abwa

Period of Imamat: 35 Years

Martyred on: 25th Rajab, 183 AH at the age of 55, poisoned by Haroon Rashid

Buried in: Kadhmain, Iraq

As all the kids packed up to leave class at the end of the period, Mrs. Hudda kept her promise and called Aliya and Sabira to come to see her.

"Sabira, do you think it was nice of you to treat Aliya that way?" she asked.

Sabira, with her head down whispered, "No, it wasn't."

Turning to Aliya, she apologized. "I'm really sorry for my attitude, Aliya. I realize it was very wrong of me to treat you that way."

Aliya gave her friend a warm hug. "It's OK, Sabira," she reassured her. "I'm sorry for being nasty with you too. I should have been more patient and acted kindly towards you."

Sabira nodded her head, "Are we friends again?" she asked hopefully.

"Most definitely! And we always will be, InshAllah!" Aliya said excitedly.

While the two girls laughed as they made up, the triangular piece in Aliya's pocket started shining. She took it out and read the words 'Kindness & Patience' on it. She showed it to Sabira and broke it into half to share with her friend. They both helped each other put it around their necks as a souvenir from the trip – a trip that had changed both of their attitudes forever.

Use this page to jot down anything you learned and that you think you can apply to your life.

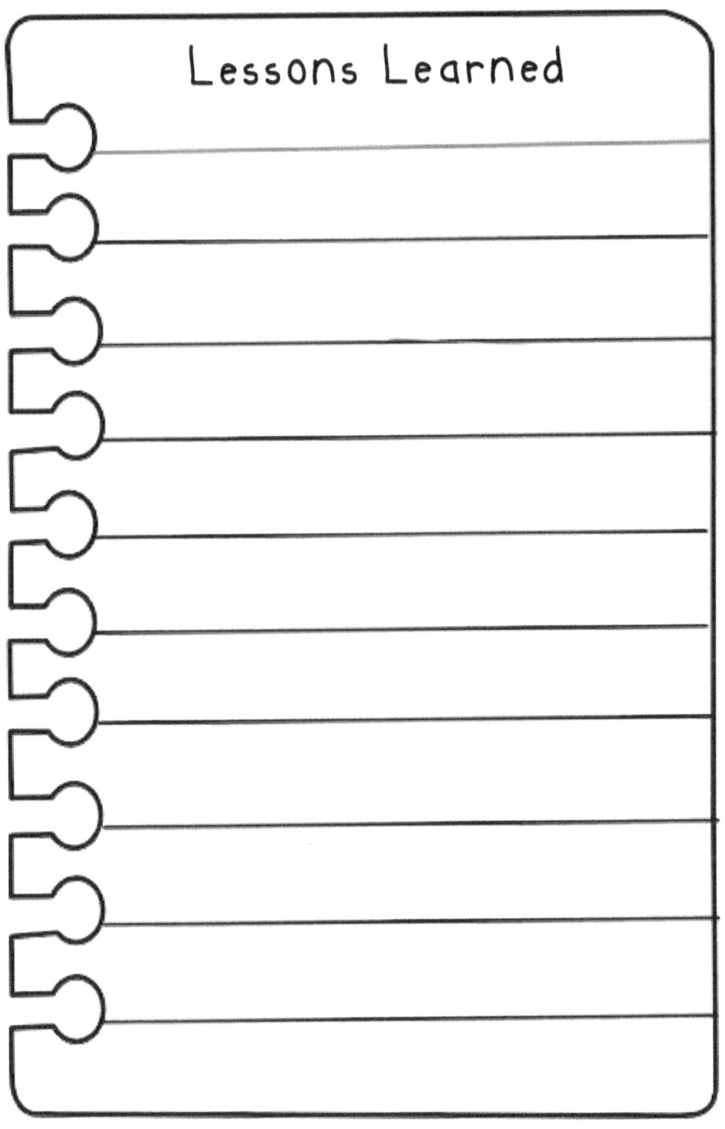

Multi-
Talented
Imam Ali ar-Ridha
(A.S)

It was early in the morning and all the students were sitting on the halaqa rug. Mrs. Hudda had a chart and on it was the structure of the human body. She was teaching them about the different bones and muscles in the human body. Without warning, Amina sneezed really loudly from the middle of the crowd. Her classmates turned to her and yelled "YarhamukumAllah!" Amina, with a smile replied, "Thank You!"

Not letting Amina's sneeze interrupt the class, Mrs. Hudda continued with her lesson on the human body. It was only a matter of seconds before Amina sneezed again.

"YarhamakumAllah!" repeated her classmates.

"Amina, would you like to get the box of tissue from your desk?" asked Mrs. Hudda. Amina didn't hesitate, and excused herself from the halaqa rug. Just as she reached for the box of tissues, she sneezed again. This time it was so loud and unexpected, that she fell down, bottom first on the floor, and all her belongings landed on top of her.

Mrs. Hudda didn't seem to find it as funny as the rest of the class did. While they chuckled and giggled, Mrs. Hudda ran to help Amina.

"Mrs. Hudda!" called out Jawaad from the halaqa rug. "It happens every spring! The weather changes and Amina starts sneezing!"

Amina nodded her head in agreement, "Jawaad is right, at this time of the year I'm like an 'Allergy Magnet'."

Mrs. Hudda looked at her, deep in thought. All of a sudden, she brightened up as if she had had a great idea and she said, "Children, did you know that the cure for allergies, flu and other sicknesses have been solved by our eighth Imam, Imam Ridha (AS)?"

From the back of the class, Hadi responded, "But Mrs. Hudda, I thought our sixth Imam was the only Imam who was into sciences."

Mrs. Hudda turned around and smiled at Hadi. "Hadi, you will be amazed to know that all our Imams were the best in all subjects! They were philosophers, doctors and scientists. Did you know that the king at the time of the eighth Imam had given Imam Ridha (AS) the title of a Doctor?"

The whole class was amazed and there were murmurs of, "Wow!" and "That's way too cool!"

Mrs. Hudda looked around the class and they noticed that mysterious twinkle in her eyes as she announced that it was time for a field trip to the past! The whole class started jumping excitedly and they followed Mrs. Hudda to the bookshelf. Mrs. Hudda carefully selected a scroll from the top shelf and opened it.

"Today we will be learning about science in Islam with the help of "Ar-Risala Dhahabiyya Fil Tibb.""

Hadi was a little taken aback. "Wow! Ar-Risalaaa a what? That is a huge Arabic word. I can't even say it, Mrs. Hudda, how am I going to understand it?" "This is the Golden Treatise or Textbook on Medicine. That's what that long Arabic name means, Hadi," clarified Mrs. Hudda.

"Okay children, it's time to go!" Mrs. Hudda and the children said,

" "LABAYK YA IMAM" "

and just as they were being zapped away, Amina had enough time to pick the triangular piece by her foot that had 'Multi-Talented' inscribed on it, and she put it in her pocket.

Mrs. Hudda and the children found themselves in a very simple and beautiful house. In the room where they were standing in, there was a table with guests already seated. Next to them were some servants, waiting for orders to serve the food.

Amina looked around and noticed that although the visitors were talking and enjoying themselves, it seemed as though they were waiting for somebody. "Mrs. Hudda, where are we? And why are these people not eating? They are just talking," asked Amina.

Mrs. Hudda explained to Amina and the other children that these people were visitors who were traveling from Khurasan and had come to have dinner with Imam Ridha (AS).

"Anybody who has dinner with the Imam is extremely lucky!" Sayyada wished she was able to dine with the Imam.

"Wow!" said Talib. "Just look at all that food, it looks scrumptious… man I'm so hungry I could eat it all… can I please, Mrs. Hudda? Can I get a bite from that table, I promise they won't know… pleaseeeeee!" He tried to run towards the table. Mrs. Hudda held him back with his collar and while restraining Talib, continued her explanation. "Children, those men who are standing next to the visitors are the servants and according to the old Arab tradition, servants never sit to eat with their masters."

Amina looked up at Mrs. Hudda and said, "Well that's not right!" Mrs. Hudda turned to Amina and smiled, "You're right, Amina, it doesn't seem fair, but just wait and see what our eighth Imam will do."

Just as Mrs. Hudda finished talking, a door opened behind them and Imam Ridha (AS) entered, surrounded by a glorious glow. The visitors stood up at the table and welcomed him. Mrs. Hudda tried to get all the children behind the large pillars, as if to give way to the Imam (AS).

Hadi, puzzled, said to Mrs. Hudda, "Nobody can see us, we don't need to move."

"Hadi, you are right, but we will get a better view of what is going to happen from here," replied Mrs. Hudda.

Imam Ridha (AS) reached the table but he didn't sit down. "Why is he not sitting down?" Talib asked out of curiosity. "Man, he had better sit down before Talib runs up and eats all the food!" laughed Jawaad.

The Holy Imam (AS) looked at the visitors and then looked at the servants. He raised his hand and invited all the servants to take a seat and dine with them. The servants were shocked, and so were the visitors. Imam Ridha (AS) repeated his gesture one more time and the servants hesitantly sat down to eat.

Amina spoke first in response to the action of the eighth Imam, "You know what Mrs. Hudda? I bet these visitors are feeling very uncomfortable eating with the servants."

Mrs. Hudda smiled at Amina. "You are probably right, but Islam believes in equality. All humans are the same; it doesn't matter if you are black, white or brown. Just look around you Amina, and you will see that just in our class, we have all types of different people, from different places. But we are all Muslims and that is the most important thing."

Jawaad snapped out of his trance and said, "Hey Mrs. Hudda, wasn't the first person who gave the Adhaan an African black slave whose name was Bilaal?"

"Yes Jawaad, I guess you have been listening in the class!" Mrs. Hudda responded with a smile.

"Now children, while everybody is having dinner on the table let me take you somewhere really special. Make a line and follow me," Mrs. Hudda continued.

The children followed Mrs. Hudda to another room that was filled with shelves of all sorts of books.

It was unbelievable! It would take forever to count the number of books in the room.

"Wow!" said Amina, stunned. "I have NEVER seen so many books in my life! I bet Imam Ridha (AS) spent a lot of time reading, this is just amazing!"

Mrs. Hudda could not help but smile at the children's astonishment. She led them to a corner of the room where there was a table. Something on the table was shining, and as they got closer Yasir couldn't contain his excitement, "Look at these coins!"

"Not just ordinary coins, Yasir. Does anybody know what's so special about them?" asked Mrs. Hudda.

Taha seemed to be deep in thought, "Well they look really old! I mean, not like the coins we have."

Jawaad gently tapped Taha on the shoulder. "Hey bro! We aren't in the 21st century here, of course they are old!" he teased his friend.

Mrs. Hudda looked at the boys and smiled at them. Amina put on her glasses and went closer to the table to look at the coins. "This is amazing! Is it just me or do these coins have the name of Imam Ridha (AS) on them?"

"You're right, Amina, the coins have the eighth Imam's name on them" Mrs. Hudda said impressed.

Sayyada felt left out. "Cheating, cheating… she has glasses so she can see things way bigger then we can."

"Haha, give me a break Sayyada, you know that isn't the truth," Amina laughed.

"I was just joking Amina, let's get back on track…" Sayyada laughed too, then asked Mrs. Hudda why Imam Ridha (AS)'s name was on the coins.

"Imam Ridha (AS) was also known as Imam Zaamin, does that sound familiar?" Mrs. Hudda asked.

"We sometimes put money towards chairty in the name of Imam Zaamin! And sometimes we also wear it on our arm when we are traveling right?" said Amir.

"That's right Amir. Zaamin comes from the words 'Zamaanat' which means safety. The King at the time of the eighth Imam made coins and put the Imam's name on it. So whenever the people who love the Masumeen wanted to travel in safety or if someone was sick, they would keep these coins with them," Mrs. Hudda added.

"But Mrs. Hudda, how can a coin help someone get better?" asked Fizza.

"They had a lot of faith and believed that the blessing of this beautiful name would help them get home safely and cure the sick. With their faith in the Imam (AS) and his connection with Allah SWT, a lot of people were helped. Remember the Masumeen have a special relationship and connection with Allah SWT. Often when we do du'a through their names and ask Allah SWT to help us for their sake, Allah SWT does so instantly if it's good for us, because He loves them so much" explained Mrs. Hudda.

"You know what Mrs. Hudda, maybe if I kept one of these coins with me, it'll make me feel better," Amina said.

"Amina, we no longer have that particular coin, but maybe you've seen your parents put some money in charity in the name of Imam Zaamin. It serves the same purpose," replied Mrs. Hudda.

Shabbir looked at the coins and suddenly spoke up. "Hey Mrs. Hudda! I have a great idea. Maybe I can take a few coins back to 21st century with me, I bet I'll make a lot of money!"

"You can't do that Shabbir because this is someone else's property, and by us taking it without permission we will be doing ghasbih," Mrs. Hudda responded.

Having had their feel of the coins, the children continued to look around the Imam's library with awe and astonishment. Sometime later, Asiya peeked out of the door and then came back to Mrs. Hudda. "Imam Ridha (AS) and his guests are all standing up and they are ready to leave. Should we follow them?" Mrs. Hudda quickly gathered everyone and told them to follow the Imam (AS).

After escorting his guests out, Imam took a book from his library, wore his black cloak and walked out of his house. The children eagerly followed him right into the palace of Mamoon.

It was the most beautiful palace the children had ever seen. The pillars, roof and walls were designed amazingly. Mrs. Hudda told everyone to stay close to her because it was very easy to get lost in this huge palace.

Imam Ridha (AS) entered the main room of the palace, where so many people were sitting and waiting. Many of the people in the audience were holding books and had several objects with them.

Amina looked around and asked with curiosity, "What's going on, Mrs. Hudda?" Before Mrs. Hudda could answer, Aliya said, "Wow! These people look so serious!"

Mrs. Hudda grinned and replied, "These are the most intelligent people of their time. There are several Physicians, Philosophers and Scientists, and please note that not all of them are Muslims, many of them are Christians."

"Wow! I had no idea we had so many intelligent Scientist and Philosophers in Islam. I also like how the different people from different religions can get together and get along!" said Jawaad.

Mrs. Hudda looked at Jawaad. "The discoveries and inventions that Muslims have contributed since the time of Prophet Adam are endless. The human race is in debt to these Muslim Scientists and our eighth Imam is the best of these Scientists and Philosophers, and yes, it's quite amazing to see how all faiths can work together - another lesson our Imams have taught us!" The children quietly found space on the floor and sat down to listen to the scientific discussions that were about to take place.

Hadi looked confused and said to nobody in particular, "I don't really understand a word they are saying, they are so clever." Amina noticed that Imam Ridha (AS) was very quiet and was intently listening to the discussion that was taking place. She turned to Mrs. Hudda and asked, "Why is the Imam so quiet? Why is he not taking part in the discussion?"

Mrs. Hudda told the children that Imam Ridha (AS) was a very intelligent man and he never spoke without being asked. Just as Mrs. Hudda finished explaining, the king of the time, Mamoon, asked the Imam if he had anything to say about all the new discoveries in science and medical healthcare.

Imam Ridha (AS) responded so eloquently. He spoke about the knowledge on medical science that he had found from his own observations and tests as well as that which he had learnt from his ancestors. He said that the information he had was so important that he would write it for all of mankind.

After the discussion finished, the children followed Imam Ridha (AS) back to his library and there they saw him write Ar-Risala Dhahabiyya Fil Tibb.

"Isn't that the scroll we traveled with?" asked Talib.

"Yes, it is" responded Mrs. Hudda

She asked all the children to sit down on the floor in the Imam's library. While he was writing the treatise, she explained to them what was going to happen next.

"Children, this is one of the most fascinating events in the history of the world. Imam Ridha (AS) after finishing the treatise, will send it to Mamoon, who will show it to many scholars and experts of his time. They will all be mesmerized with the teachings of Imam Ridha (AS). This treatise will be highly praised and written in gold, and that is how it will get the name: 'The Golden Treatise of Medicine'."

"What is written in the treatise, Mrs. Hudda?" asked Sumayya.

"The treatise talks about how to protect your body from diseases and how to enjoy perfect health. It also gives information on certain ways of keeping your body fit."

"Hey, that's like what these doctors do when we go to see them. They show you what is wrong with you and how you can get rid of it," added Jawaad.

"Yes, Jawaad. The second part of the treatise

is about the importance of bathing and how it helps your health. It also talks about the nutrients and food you should eat to have a healthy body" continued Mrs. Hudda.

"Wow! I love our Imams," exclaimed Hadi. "They are truly blessed by Allah SWT. They knew so much and we didn't even realize it! Where can we get copies of the Golden treatise of Medicine?"

Mrs. Hudda looked at Hadi, thinking about his question. "You know what Hadi? That is a very good question. When you go back to the classroom, you can look over the scroll we used to travel. You can also look through the school library and you will find books that contain parts of the treatise."

"Yeah I will! This is the coolest thing ever" he replied. "Okay everyone. It's time to go!" Mrs. Hudda said. The children gathered together and put their hands on the scroll and said "LABAYK YA IMAM." They reached the class with just enough time for a discussion on the halaqa rug.

The children sat in a circle and Mrs. Hudda asked them what they had learnt from their trip to the past. As they discussed their new discoveries, they copied down the basic facts on Imam Ridha.

Name: Ali

Title: Ar-Ridha (the one who was content), Imam Zaamin

Father: Imam Musa Kadhim

Mother: Najma

Birthday : 11 Dhul Qad 148 AH

Born in Medina

Imam for 20 years

Died on the 29th of Safar 203 AH at the age of 55 Mamoon Rashid poisoned the Imam with grapes

Buried in Mashad Iran

Interesting Fact: wrote Al Risala Al Dhahabiyya Fil Tibb

While they were copying, Hadi suddenly had a thought. "Imam Ridha (AS) showed us there is no difference in people, we are all the same and therefore we should not look down at anyone as we are all creatures of Allah SWT."

"Yeah, that's right! I also learnt about the coin of Imam Zaamin and how we ask Allah SWT for help and our needs through the Imams, and if it's good for us, out of His love for them, our prayers will be answered quicker," shared Jawaad.

Amina clutched the triangular piece in her pocket tightly and said, "Islam is known for its scientific discoveries and Islam is not only about religion but also secular education, like science. Our Imams were the best Philosophers, Scientists and Physicians ever to walk on this planet. If you really study Islam, you are studying everything and are multi-talented. Not only do you learn about religion, but also about the different subjects we learn about in school."

Mrs. Hudda ended the class discussion by asking, "Did you all enjoy the field trip?" The children responded enthusiastically, "Yes we did, Mrs. Hudda!"

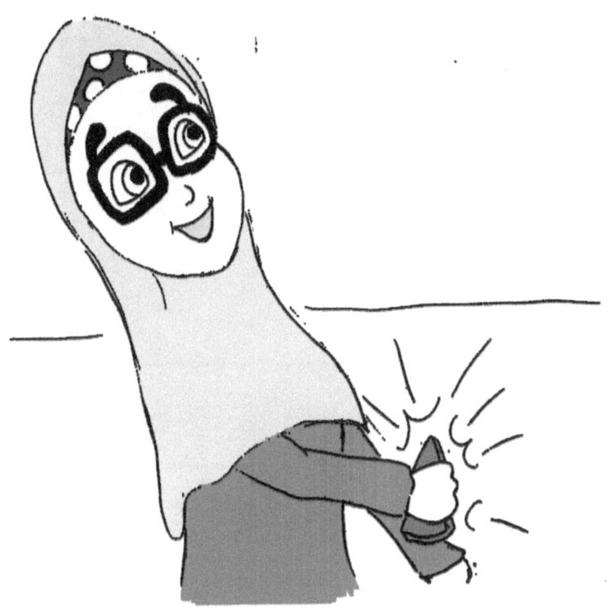

"Aahhhhchooooooo!" Without any warning, Amina sneezed really loudly. She ran to her desk, took out some change and put it in the Imam Zamin charity box and asked Allah SWT to cure her allergies.

As the bell rang and the children left the class, Amina whispered to Mrs. Hudda that she was going to keep a coin with the intention of Imam Zaamin with her always, and that she had full faith that the eighth Imam would pray to Allah SWT to help her get better. She also would pray that someday she would be a doctor, just like he was inshAllah!

Use this page to jot down anything you learned and that you think you can apply to your life.

Lessons Learned

Selflessness
Imam Muhammed al-Jawad (A.S)

Hadi and Taha walked towards Class 786 at Al-Iman Madrassah. "Watch where you go, kiddo!" an older kid shouted as Hadi walked into him by mistake, almost knocking his books out of his hand. Hadi and Taha paid no attention to him. They were busy counting the money in their hands – and rummaging for extra change in their pockets.

"I made fourteen dollars this week. That's pretty decent, eh?" Hadi gloated.

"My dad only gave me ten this week" Taha said in a disappointed tone.

"Well, see… Dads are like that. They only give you the money that you earn. It's not that easy to make money as a nine year old, you know? I had to mow the lawn and wash the car over the weekend. I also did tons of chores at home throughout the rest of the week. You know what though? All that is so worth it, coz at the end of the week Daddy gives me my allowance!" Hadi rambled on as Taha started counting his money again to make sure he had counted it right.

They found their seats as they walked into class and continued discussing the important financial issues that shaped the life of a nine year old. A few minutes later, they were distracted by the sudden calm that surrounded the classroom. When they looked up, they noticed Mrs. Hudda entering the classroom. "That's a beautiful ring, Mrs. Hudda!" Asiya exclaimed. "I've never seen that before… what's that star shape design on it?"

"Hirz of Imam Jawad (AS)," Mrs. Hudda responded. "It is a ring with a du'a inside that protects the one who wears it from every calamity except death."

"Oh… wow!" Shabbir exclaimed.

"Are we going to learn about the ninth Imam today?" Jawaad asked.

"That was a very good guess, Jawaad!" Mrs. Hudda smiled at Jawaad. The kids saw Mrs. Hudda arranging the halaqa rug and joined her on it. She took the ring off her finger and placed it in the middle of the circle. The class focused on the ring as they said "LABAYK YA IMAM" in unison.

Hadi suddenly noticed a triangular piece in his right hand. He read the word 'Selflessness' engraved on it. He put the piece in his pocket and chanted "LABAYK YA IMAM" the second time with the class. The entire class was then zapped back in time to a street in Medina.

The children were overjoyed at the sight of the lively street with kids from the entire neighborhood playing all sorts of outdoor games together. Suddenly, they felt the ground shaking and vibrating.

"Ya Allah!" Aliya exclaimed. "This reminds me of when the dinosaurs came into the city in Jurassic Park!" Everyone looked at her like she was nuts! "We haven't gone THAT far back in time, Aliya!" Taha retorted. The class turned around to see a huge entourage of horses and horsemen approaching them. All the neighborhood kids ran away at the sight of the horsemen. Even the kids from Class 786 tried to find bushes to hide behind, despite knowing they could not be seen! When the entire street was deserted, the class noticed that one young boy had not moved from his place.

The group of horsemen stopped as they neared the young boy. The man at the very front of the group was dressed in a royal, bright robe and had a crown on his head. It only took the class a few minutes to realize that this must be one of the so-called Caliphs of the time. Mrs. Hudda informed them that the Caliph's name was Mamoon Rashid – the same Caliph who poisoned Imam Ridha(AS).

He approached the young boy, and asked, "Young man, why did you not run away like the other children?"

The young boy confidently responded, "Neither had I committed a crime, nor was I blocking the way. Why should I have run away or be afraid? I also know that you will not cause any unnecessary trouble when your way is not blocked."

Surprised by the mature reply of a boy of such tender age, Mamoon asked his name.

"Muhammed," responded the boy.

"Whose son are you?" Mamoon further questioned him.

"Son of Ali ibn Musa," the young boy responded calmly.

The class gasped at hearing that. "That young boy is our Imam!" they screamed in unison. "That's brave of him to stand up to the Caliph like that even though he is so young!" Taha said in admiration.

Mamoon realizing that this was a member of the household of the Holy Prophet (SAW) and not some random kid who he could scare with his majesty and pomp, rode on to continue his hunting trip. When Mamoon's hunting trip was over, he returned to the city of Medina on his way back to the capital. Mamoon's hawk returned to him with a fish in its beak. He again noticed that all the neighborhood kids ran away at the sight of his entourage except the ninth Imam. He approached the young boy again and asked him, "Tell me, what is there in my fist?"

"God created clouds between the earth and sky. The hawks of kings sometimes catch fish and bring it to the kings. They hide it in their fist and ask a member of the Ahlul Bayt of the Prophet, 'Tell me, what is there in my fist?'" responded Imam Muhammed at-Taqi al-Jawad (AS) intelligently.

"Truly, you are the worthy son of

Ali ibn Musa ar-Ridha!" Mamoon exclaimed, astounded by the intelligence of the Imam at such a young age. The kids turned around to form a circle and talk about the courage the Imam had to stand up for himself and the truth. They noticed the day transforming into the night. In the dark night, the Hirz of Imam Jawad (AS) began to glow and the kids were zapped into the future. They found themselves in the palace of Mamoon Rashid.

Mamoon was telling his Abbasid chiefs that he had decided to offer his daughter, Ummul Fadhl, in marriage to the ninth Imam. When the chiefs questioned his decision, he tried to convince them of the Imam's nobility. In addition to being from the progeny of the Holy Prophet (SAW), Imam Jawad (AS) had inherited all the admirable traits and virtues from his father.

Finally the chiefs and Mamoon reached an agreement. They would have the most knowledgeable elders of the city meet with the Imam and test his knowledge. If Mamoon was proved right, he would give his daughter in marriage to the Imam. The gathering was arranged and one of the most notable scholars, Yahya, was

summoned to ask Imam the most difficult of questions.

Yahya asked the Imam, "What is the repayment for a person who hunts an animal while in the state of Ihram?" Yahya was gloating with pride at the difficulty of the question he had posed. The Imam on the other hand, calmly replied. "Your question is utterly vague and lacks definition. You should first clarify whether the animal killed was outside the sanctified area or inside it; whether the hunter was aware of his sin or did it in ignorance; did he kill the animal purposely or by mistake; was the hunter a slave or a free man; was he an adult or a minor; did he commit the sin for the first time or had he done so before; was the hunted animal a bird or something else; was it a small animal or a big one; is the sinner sorry for doing the wrong thing or does he think he is right; did he kill it secretly at night or openly during daylight; was he putting on the Ihram for Hajj or for the Umrah? Unless you clarify and define these aspects, how can you have a definite answer?"

Yahya was astonished at the intelligence of the Imam. He realized that as clever as he was, there was no competition between him and the Imam of the time who was from the progeny of the

Holy Prophet (SAW). He went on to accept his defeat when he failed to answer a question the Imam put forward to him.

Mamoon, seeing the outcome of this gathering told his chiefs, "Did I not tell you that the people of the Ahlul Bayt of the Prophet have been gifted by Allah SWT with unlimited knowledge?"

He then offered Ummul Fadhl's hand in marriage to the Imam. He had heard the predictions that the twelfth Imam was going to be born from the 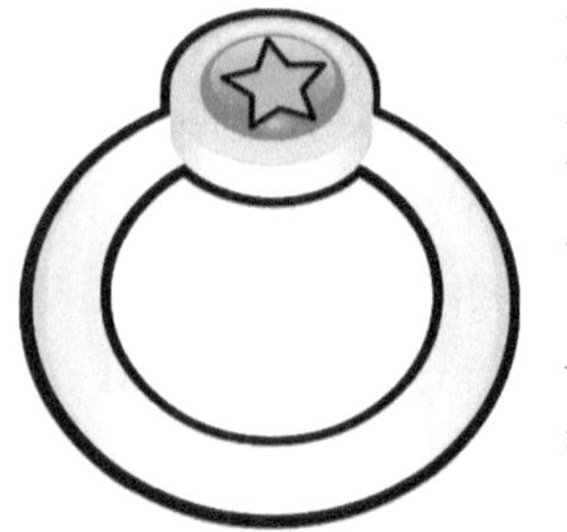 progeny of this Imam. He really wanted that Imam to be born from his daughter because that would give the Abbasid Empire legitimacy and pride.

The Hirz of Imam Jawad began to glow as everything surrounding the children started to fade away. They found themselves in the palace of Mamoon Rashid again. "Ummul Fadhl was a very demanding and controlling woman. She was always eager to give Imam Jawad (AS) a hard time and hurt him," Mrs. Hudda explained as the children saw a woman march into the palace of Mamoon.

A surprised Mamoon exclaimed, "What brings you here in such a state, my daughter?!"

"Your plan has failed, my father!" she shouted. "You had married me to Muhammed ibn Ali ar-Ridha in the hope that I would bear him a child that would be the next Imam."

"What do you mean? How has my plan failed?" Mamoon asked desperately.

"He has a wife and a son in Medina," Ummul Fadhl told him angrily.

As Mamoon's face turned red with rage, the surroundings started to fade away and the ring began to glow.

The children found themselves outside the house of the Imam and saw an angry and drunken Mamoon approaching the house. As Mamoon left the house a few minutes later, he was muttering under his breath in fear. In his drunken and angry state, he had attacked the Imam and tried to kill him. Now, he was was planning on how to bury his body so that nobody would find out that he had killed him.

Overtaken by sadness, the children sat down

outside the house of the Imam. As the sun began to rise the next day, they saw Mamoon approaching the house again. With surprise and joy, they also

saw Imam Jawad (AS) coming out of the house, without as much as a single scratch on his body.

"I thought I killed you!" Mamoon exclaimed in surprise. "What saved your life?"

The Imam showed Mamoon the amulet he was wearing. It resembled the amulet on the ring Mrs. Hudda wore. "This amulet was given to me by my grandmother, Fatema Zahra (AS)," Imam Jawad (AS) began to explain, "it protects the one who wears it from everything except the Angel of

Death, when it is their time to go."

The kids turned to look at the amulet on Mrs. Hudda's ring in amazement. They now realized how it had gotten the name of Hirz of Imam Jawad (AS) – because it had been introduced to us by the ninth Imam whose title was Jawad.

The amulet began to glow and the children clustered closer together and were zapped back into the classroom.

Everyone quickly took out their notebooks and found a spot on the halaqa rug. They copied down the information Mrs. Hudda wrote on the board.

Imam Jawad was so clever and brave! Even when he was just a kid he stood up to the ruler of the time. He did not think of himself all the time and helped other people with his wealth and knowledge. I am going to try and give a little of my hard-earned pocket money to charity, and a bit of advice to my brother!

Name: Muhammed

Title: At-Taqi (The Pious) and Al-Jawad (The Generous)

Father: Imam Ali ar-Ridha (AS)

Mother: Khaizran Khatoon

Birthday: 10th Rajab 193 AH

Lived for: 25 Years

Martyred on: 29th Dhul-Qida 220AH, poisoned by: Mu'tasim, the Abbasid King

Buried in: Kadhmain, Iraq.

While all the children were busy noting down the facts from the board, the triangular piece in Hadi's pocket began to glow. He took it out and read the word 'Selflessness' engraved on it.

"The Imam was very selfless," Hadi thought out loud. "Even though he was surrounded by so much wealth and riches, he continued to live a life of simplicity."

"I noticed that too," Taha said in agreement. "He was married to the Caliph's daughter – he could easily have had all the wealth and money he wanted. But the material things meant nothing to him. There's much more to life than money, I guess."

"Like all our Imams, Imam Jawad (AS) was very brave as well," Asiya added. "I couldn't believe how he stood up to the Caliph at such a young age!"

Mrs. Hudda smiled at the children. They had learnt so much from their adventures in the past eleven weeks. She could see they were getting ready to experience the adventure on their fourteenth week – after all, these weekly adventures were meant to prepare them for the final experience that they would remember for the rest of their lives!

Use this page to jot down anything you learned and that you think you can apply to your life.

Truthful
Imam Ali an-Naqi
(A.S)

As the bell of Al-Iman Madrassah rang, children scattered from the hallways. For Class 786, it was another day of adventures. As the children settled into their seats, Yasir ran up to Mrs. Hudda who was writing on the chalk board.

"Mrs. Hudda! This is not fair! Sayyada stole my pencil!" "No I did not!" retorted Sayyada confidently, as she rushed up to Mrs. Hudda's desk behind Yasir.

Mrs. Hudda looked at the two students bickering back and forth. "Children!" she said in a stern voice. "We will sort this out after class; right now it is time to begin the lesson."

She looked at all of her students and noticed many of them wearing their triangular pieces from their past adventures around their necks. "Just a few more pieces of the puzzle to go and inshAllah we will go on our trip," She whispered to herself. She then turned her attention completely towards the class and began by greeting them. Imran had overheard Mrs. Hudda, and a puzzled look formed on his face. He wondered where they might go. "I hope she doesn't mean to Mr. Hashim's office!" he thought, dreading the prospect.

"Salaamun alaykum, Mrs. Hudda!" the kids enthusiastically greeted her. No lesson in Class 786 was a normal boring lesson, and the students knew that only too well. Mrs. Hudda walked towards the bookshelf and began to explain, "Every week we have been learning about the life of one of the fourteen Masumeen. Today we are going to learn about the tenth Imam. Who knows the name of the tenth Imam?"

"Our tenth Imam is Imam Ali an-Naqi (AS)!" Sayyada quickly responded.

"Excellent, Sayyada!" complimented Mrs. Hudda. "And who is his father?"

Hadi threw his hand in the air. "The ninth Imam! Imam Muhammed at-Taqi al-Jawad (AS)."

"Wasn't his mother Sumanna Khatoon?" asked Asiya.

Talib, feeling the class's excitement and enthusiasm, also wanted to share what he knew. "I know he was born on the 15th of Zillhajj, and he died on the 3rd of Rajab, at the age of 42."

Mrs. Hudda could not help but smile; she was very impressed with her students. Fizza noticed how joyful Mrs. Hudda was. "Mrs. Hudda, we are trying to follow the footsteps of our Masumeen. The Holy Prophet (SAW) said that reading and seeking knowledge is really important, so we try to read before we come to class, that's why we know so much more than before!"

Mrs. Hudda's smile widened at the warm faces looking at her. She was very proud of her students and she continued to explain more about Imam Ali an-Naqi (AS).

"Just like our other Imams, the tenth Imam also faced many difficulties, but do you know that he was very famous?" continued Mrs. Hudda.

The children's eyes widened in amazement. "Famous? Really? For what?" they asked.

"He spread the message of Islam, and taught the people the difference between right and wrong, and about Allah SWT. People were inspired by what he would say, and whenever he talked about religion, they gathered around him" explained Mrs. Hudda.

Jawaad remembered something his mom had told him, "Didn't the tenth Imam also spend time in prison?"

Mrs. Hudda nodded. She then headed towards the bookshelf, but this time she didn't reach for a book; instead she took out a prayer mat from the bottom shelf.

"The Imam was known for his prayers. Even when the enemy broke into his house, they saw him praying in a corner."

Yasir looked at the triangular piece around his neck that had the word 'Salaat' engraved on it and realized that all the Masumeen had very similar characteristics and that salaat was very important. The children got up from their desks and rushed towards Mrs. Hudda. They had seen the mysterious twinkle in her eyes and they knew it was the sign of time travel! They all grabbed a part of the prayer mat and chanted,

Sayyada saw a clay piece fall out of the prayer mat. She quickly picked it up, read the words 'Truthful' and put it in her pocket. As the children looked around, they noticed that they had been zapped back to the time of Mutawakkil, the Abbasid ruler at the time of the tenth Imam.

The children saw a lady, and Mrs. Hudda told them to follow her. They followed the lady and soon found themselves in the court of Mutawakkil. She said:

Mutawakkil looked baffled, "Surely you cannot be Zainab! Many years have passed since she was alive, and you are a young lady."

"I am Zainab!" the lady insisted. "I am young because the Holy Prophet (SAW) passed his hand over my head and prayed that I remain young forever!"

"I do not believe you!" Mutawakkil retorted.

Mrs. Hudda pointed towards an area near the throne, and whispered to the children, "Do you see the group of people sitting there?"

The children nodded. "Who are they?" asked Yasir.

"Those are the wise men. Those are the men that Mutawakkil calls when he has a problem," Mrs. Hudda replied.

"Look! He's calling them now!" Hadi interrupted.

"He is confused! He doesn't believe the lady, so now is he going to ask those men for help?" Talib asked as Mutawakkil started to speak.

"What do you think? You are the wisest men of this time, do you think this lady is lying?" asked Mutawakkil.

The man sitting closest to him responded, "I don't think she is telling the truth." "She is lying! How can she be Zainab?" added another of the wise men. "But how are we going to prove that she is wrong?" responded his friend who sat beside him.

Everybody in the court knew, though they were not too eager to admit, that there was nobody truly wiser than the Imam of their time, who was the tenth Imam. Even Mutawakkil, who claimed to have all the power, knew that the Imam had an answer to everything.

Mutawakkil was so confused that he made a decision. "Let us call Ali an-Naqi! He can definitely help us prove that what this lady is saying is not true."

The children watched as a few of Mutawakkil's men left the court and headed towards the Imam's house.

Not too long after, they returned with the tenth Imam. There was a heavenly light surrounding the Imam. The children's hearts felt peace and they smiled, it was the same warm feeling they had felt in their previous adventures. The Imam was so humble and pious, like the other Masumeen.

Mutawakkil had been anxiously waiting for the Imam, and as he entered, Mutawakkil began to speak, "Ali! This lady has come here saying she is Zainab, the daughter of Fatema Zahra, and the granddaughter of Muhammed. We do not believe her, but how do we prove that what she is saying is not true?"

Imam Ali an-Naqi (AS) was very composed and he calmly responded, "Put this lady in a cage of lions. If what she is saying is true, then the lions will not harm her, because the creatures of Allah SWT do not hurt the children of Fatema Zahra."

The lady began to tremble, and fear was all over her face. "Do you want to kill me? If what you are saying is true, and you claim to be the Imam, then why don't you enter the cage first?"

Imam Ali an-Naqi (AS) did not hesitate to answer, "I am an Imam, and the great grandson of the lady of Light, Fatma Zahra. I will enter the cage of lions before you."

The children seemed curious as to what was going to happen next, but they had seen how brave the other Masumeen were and knew that they only spoke the truth. Even when people challenged them they were not afraid because they had Allah SWT on their side, and they were firm on the right path.

The children watched as a cage with lions was brought into the court of Mutawakkil. The lady was persistent and just as curious as the children. She spoke sarcastically, "Oh you who claim that you are the Imam! Enter the cage."

A few of the children turned away; it was not that the children didn't trust the Imam, they just couldn't bear to look.

Asiya closed her eyes and covered them with her hands, peeking through the tiny gaps between her fingers. A part of her knew he was the true Imam, but another part of her was a bit scared. There was a deadly silence in the court as the Imam confidently entered the cage of lions.

"You can open your eyes now Asiya!" said Jawad, with some encouragement.

"Look in the cage, the lions aren't harming the Imam!" Imam Ali an-Naqi (AS) was gently stroking the lions as they approached him and humbly sat beside him. "This is amazing!" said Asiya, feeling a great relief.

"The lions will not harm me, as I am from the family of the Ahlul Bayt," said the Imam, "Now it is your turn," he turned to the lady.

She began to cry, "I am so sorry! I was only joking! I just wanted to see how Mutawakkil would respond! I did not mean to lie, I'm so sorry."

Sayyada felt guilty as she pondered over what she just saw. Hadi knew what she was thinking and said to her, "We should never lie, even if it is a joke. Allah SWT knows everything and He will punish us if we lie."

Mrs. Hudda acknowledged Hadi's statement. "That's right Hadi, but also remember that Allah SWT is so merciful and loves us very much. He doesn't want to punish us so He gives us many chances to ask for forgiveness. If you are sorry for what you did and promise not to do it again, He will inshAllah forgive you. Always remember Allah SWT loves you, and always ask for forgiveness when you do things that He doesn't like. Let's follow the Imam, there is still so much more to learn from his actions and words."

Sayyada hugged Mrs. Hudda and softly prayed to Allah SWT to forgive her. The children then followed Mrs. Hudda out of the court, behind the Imam. As they were walking in the streets, a man who looked a bit worried and stressed, approached Imam Ali an-Naqi (AS). The children stopped dead in their tracks, eager to listen to the conversation between the Imam and the worried man.

The worried man began to speak, "Oh Imam! I am seeking your help! Please help me, if you don't help me I will be killed!"

The Imam responded calmly, "Oh young man, please do explain, what is it that you seek help for?"

The man began telling the Imam of his problem. "The king! He gave me a very expensive stone and he told me to engrave something on it. But when I went to write on it, the stone broke in half! The king is going to order his men to kill me! What shall I do?"

"Young man, please do not worry, I am praying for you, please do not worry, Allah SWT will surely look after you," responded Imam an-Naqi (AS).

"Thank you, my Imam!" the man exclaimed, relieved and trusting in the Imam's word.

As the man headed down the street, the children followed him back to his shop, curious to see what was going to happen next. A little while later, the king walked into the man's shop with his guards. The anxious man remembered the words of the Imam, yet he was still worried and scared.

The king began to speak, "Young man, I have changed my mind. I would like you to break that expensive stone I have given you into two pieces. I have two daughters and I would like each of my daughters to have a piece, please write on each half of the stone."

The young man responded shakily, "Yes, your Majesty." He could not believe what he was hearing. As relief washed over him, he thanked Allah SWT from the bottom of his heart.

Fizza couldn't keep it in anymore, "Wow! The Imam prayed for this man, and that changed the king's mind!"

Mrs. Hudda began to explain, "The man did not have bad intentions, the stone broke by accident and so Allah SWT helped him. What is the Imam teaching us here?"

"We should always speak the truth and have faith in Allah SWT!" Haider answered.

"Always ask for Allah SWT's help, because He will always help us," added Sumayya.

"And don't forget the power of intercession, the power of our Imams praying for us! Allah SWT loves them so much, and listens to their prayers faster!" gleamed Amina.

Mrs. Hudda had tears in her eyes, the children were really learning. "You are all so right. We have one more stop before we go back to the classroom. The house of Imam an-Naqi (AS) is not far from here." The children walked with excitement and talked about the incident they had just witnessed. It was unbelievable! They arrived at the house of the tenth Imam and peered through the window. They saw the Imam talking to a lady. Mrs. Hudda told them that the lady was the mother of Mutawakkil. The children pressed their ears to the window to hear the conversation.

The mother of Mutawakkil looked very upset as she spoke to the Imam. "Oh Imam! My son, Mutawakkil, is very ill. The doctors say they can't make him better. Please, is there anything you can do to help him?"

Imam an-Naqi (AS) got up and left the room. He returned shortly after and gave the lady some medicine. "Give this medicine to your son, he will become better soon, InshAllah." As she left the house she thanked the Imam.

"Mutawakkil is sick, maybe the lions bit him!" joked Jawaad.

Mrs. Hudda sighed at Jawaad's joke. "Boys will always be boys," she thought to herself. She then explained that the medicine the Imam gave helped Mutawakkil get better and all the doctors were surprised.

Ammar looked preoccupied. Something was bothering him and he couldn't keep it bottled up anymore. "Mrs. Hudda, why did the Imam help Mutawakkil if he was a bad man?"

"The Imam was teaching us that if anybody ever asks you for help, you should help them, even if they are not nice," Mrs. Hudda replied.

"Wow, our Masumeen really are great people!" Sabira exclaimed.

Mrs. Hudda pulled out the prayer mat. The children held onto it and with a flash of light, they were back in the classroom.

It was time to recap the day's lesson.

The children rushed to the halaqa rug and began to copy information from the board as they discussed what they had learnt. They were all fascinated with the lion story and kept talking about it. It had been the highlight of the day's lesson.

Name: Ali

Title: al-Hadi (The Guide)
       an-Naqi (The Pure)

Father: Imam Muhammed al-
        Jawad

Mother: Sumanna Khatoon

Birthday: 15th Zil Hajj 212 AH

Born in Medina

Imam for 33 Years

Died at the age of 42 on the 3rd
of Rajab, 254 AH, poisoned by
Mut'az Ababasid Caliph

Buried in Samarra Iraq

Mrs. Hudda noticed Sayyada approaching Hadi in a corner of the classroom. She could barely hear, but she heard enough to make her happy.

Sayyada lowered her head, feeling a little guilty,

"I'm really sorry, Hadi. I did take your pencil because I liked it. I learnt when we saw that lady lying that I shouldn't lie, and how Allah SWT helps honest people like the stone cutter. I'm sorry."

"That's okay, I forgive you," Hadi responded humbly.

Sayyada noticed her pocket glowing, she took out the triangular piece that she had picked up earlier and put it around her neck. "I promise you, Allah SWT, that I will try to always speak the truth."

"Ilaahi Ameen," whispered Mrs. Hudda as the final bell for the day rang. The children all yelled 'Fi Ammanillah' to Mrs. Hudda as they packed their backpacks and raced out the class, eager to share what they learned in Madressah with their family and friends.

Use this page to jot down anything you learned and that you think you can apply to your life.

Stay in Touch
with Imam
Imam Hassan
al-Askari (A.S)

It was a gloomy day as the students of Class 786 headed to class. As they walked in they saw Mrs. Hudda sobbing sitting next to the television. Her eyes and cheeks were puffy as if someone she loved dearly had passed away or something really bad had happened to someone she cared a lot about.

Sayyada took out a tissue from her purse, ran towards Mrs. Hudda and gently wiped the tears off from her flushed cheeks. Something strange happened, everyone started to tear up as their eyes were glued to the television screen. Their tiny hearts felt like they were cracking as they heard:

"This just in, there has been a bomb explosion in the Askarian Shrine in Samarra. The Askarian Shrine is the holy place where the tenth and eleventh Imam of the Ahlul Bayt are buried. Imam Hassan al-Askari was born in Medina on the 10th of Rabi al-Akhar and died in Samarra, Iraq on 8th of Rabi al-Awwal at the age of 28. This is truly a devastating, heartbreaking day for all the people who love the family of the Prophet around the world. Our condolences to his son, the Imam of our time…"

As the news report showed pictures of the destruction of the shrine, the children could not take it anymore. They all sat in a circle, took out the Sahifa as-Sajjadiyah from the fourth Imam and started to read the dua for when one is sad. The dua helped ease their hearts and they all knew they had to go back in time to learn more about their eleventh Imam.

Imran was a bit fidgety, "Mrs. Hudda I want to make a card for Imam Mahdi to say sorry but I don't know his address, do you?" Mrs. Hudda pulled herself together and hugged Imran. She told all the children to gather around and hold on to this piece of paper; it was a plain white paper with some Arabic on the top and some Arabic on the bottom. As each one grabbed a part of the paper, they all chanted,

" "LABAYK YA IMAM" "

Imran noticed a clay triangular piece fall from the back of the paper which said 'Stay in touch with the Imam.' He put it in his pocket and joined his peers. Before they knew it they were back in time, in the land of Baghdad where they saw Imam Hassan Askari (AS) in jail.

Mrs. Hudda saw the confused faces and started to explain. "The evil rulers of the time were worried about the Holy Prophet (SAW)'s hadith, that there would be twelve divinely appointed successors after him and that the twelfth one would fill the world with justice just as it was filled with oppression."

"These people were scared and wanted to ensure that the twelfth Imam was never born, so they put the tenth Imam in prison or under house arrest for long periods of time. After the tenth Imam was martyred, the people were even more scared as they knew that the eleventh Imam would be the father of the twelfth, so Imam Hassan Askari (AS) also spent most of his life in prison or under house arrest."

Jawaad was angry. "What's up with these evil rulers, why can't they just leave our Imams alone? Man what a bunch of losers!" "Here comes one of those losers now!" Fizza interrupted Jawaad, as she pointed to a solider approaching Imam Hassan Askari's jail cell.

The solider opened the jail cell and informed Imam Hassan Askari (AS) that the Caliph Mutamid wanted him to come to the palace. He grabbed the Imam and led him to the palace. When Mutamid saw Imam Hassan Askari (AS), he began talking.

"There is a severe draught. Rain has not fallen for some time and crops are drying up. People are facing a famine. Just the other day a Christian priest came to the rescue. He lifted his hands in prayer and it rained. I fear people will leave Islam and become Christians. The priest will be coming again, what should I do?"

"When the people are gathered to see the so-called miracle performed by the Christian priest, let me be present. I will remove their doubts," Imam Hassan Askari (AS) calmly replied.

Mutamid was desperate and agreed. "You will be allowed to leave the prison to go where the crowd is assembled to see the miracle performed by the priest. Guards, take him to the town square."

"Look how humble and pious our Imam is, that evil ruler puts him in jail and he still helps him. It's a characteristic of all our Masumeen," thought Yasir.

The children followed them to the town square and watched as Imam Hassan Askari (AS) stood with the crowd and watched the priest raise his hands to pray and it started raining again. Imam Hassan Askari (AS) told the guards to look at what the priest was holding and bring the piece of bone hidden in his hands.

Imam Hassan Askari (AS) held the bone up high to show everyone and explained, "This is the bone of a Prophet of Allah SWT. It was the effect of this holy bone, when lifted in prayers to Allah SWT, that brought Allah SWT's mercy and brought rain to the land." 

The crowd was shocked. Imam Hassan Askari (AS) then spread his prayer mat and performed two rak'ats of prayers. He then lifted his bare hands to Allah SWT for rain to come to the land and wipe out the drought. The students of Class 786 started to run for cover, because Imam Hassan Askari (AS)'s prayer was heard by the Almighty and so much rain fell that the land became fertile again and crops began to grow. As they all ran back to the palace, Mutamid was relieved but now was worried about another issue.

He thought to himself, "What will the people think of me if I imprison this man?!" He looked at Imam Hassan Askari (AS) and said, "For what you did, you are allowed to leave the prison and live in your house in Samarra under house arrest. My guards will be watching your every move."

"MashAllah - that was a miracle, the miracle that set the path to the birth of Imam Mahdi (AS)! It says in the Qur'an, 'And they planned and Allah (also) planned, and Allah is the best of planners' Truly, Allah's will always happens," Imran shared as he beamed with happiness.

The children continued to walk behind Imam Hasan Askari (AS) to his house. Imran scratched his head and with a puzzled look wondered, "Mrs. Hudda, Allah SWT promises that He will never leave His creation without a guide. How is it possible for the people in the time of Imam Hassan Askari (AS) to keep in touch with him if Mutamid is watching his every step? Just like me - I can't even email the twelfth Imam a condolence card."

"Oh Imran, Allah SWT always keeps His promise. Watch and see," Mrs. Hudda said as she comforted Imran.

As days went by the children watched Imam Hassan Askari (AS) living his life under house arrest. They were amazed to see how, despite being under house arrest, Imam Hassan Askari (AS) conducted his duties as Imam from inside the house. Through letters and students who were allowed to visit him he spread the message of Islam. He helped people who had problems. He taught people Qur'an and instructed his followers the true teachings of Islam as taught by the Prophet of Islam and his Ahlul Bayt.

The children watched as Imam Hassan Askari wrote a complete Tafseer of the Qur'an, using his abundant knowledge and the time he had.

Imran started to get the feeling that Allah SWT always keeps His promise, but was still a bit doubtful.

They were about to get ready to be transported back, when they saw the wife of Imam Hassan Askari (AS), Lady Narjis Khatoon, go to Imam Hassan Askari (AS) in pain. Imam Hassan Askari took her into the room and a few hours later the children saw a bundle in his arms, it was a baby boy!

Sumayya started to shiver, "Is that, is that, is thaaattt…. Imam Mahdi (AS)?!"

Mrs. Hudda nodded. "Look at the baby. Like all the other eleven Imams he is born clean with no impurity or defects. Look between his shoulders, there is a seal of the Imams imprinted by Allah SWT."

"Look, he is doing sajdah," pointed Sabira.

"Now he is looking at the sky and is reciting the Kalima," whispered Taha.

"And the names of all the Masumeen before him," added Aliya.

The children watched contently as Imam Hassan Askari (AS) read the Adhan and Iqama in his ears. They knew this baby was the one who will bring justice to the world.

"I can't believe we just saw the birth of Imam Mahdi (AS), did you see how happy Imam Hassan Askari was?" shared Aliya.

Mrs. Hudda explained to the children that soon after Imam Mahdi (AS) was born, Imam Hassan Askari (AS), with Allah SWT's guidance, sent him away for protection. Five years later, Imam Hassan

Askari was back in prison and Mutamid poisoned him to death.

As the news of the Imam's death spread in Samarra, the markets became deserted. Banu Hashim, the military officers, the state secretaries, the judges, and the members of the public all attended his funeral. On that day there was a major void in Samarra as there was no one among them who was more distinguished than Imam Hassan al-Askari. He was the best in knowledge, piety, humbleness, dignity, nobility, modesty and honesty. With tears in their eyes, the children arrived back to their classroom. On every desk there was a piece of paper, similar to the one they had used to transport themselves with.

"Imran, you are glowing!!" Fizza shouted. Imran looked at the triangular piece in his hand that was glowing. He smiled and read it out loud, 'Stay in touch with the Imam'.

Mrs. Hudda explained to the children that even though we cannot see our twelfth Imam, Imam Mahdi (AS), we can communicate with him like the people communicated with the eleventh Imam.

"Allah SWT promised that He would never leave us without a guide, and our guide is Imam

Mahdi (AS). An aridha is a special letter that we write to our Imam; in it we write our wishes and our problems. We then take that aridha and throw it in the ocean or bury it, asking Imam's third messenger during his minor occultation, Hussian ibn Ruh, to take it to the Imam for us. So Imran, Imam Madhi (AS)'s address is an ocean, a lake, the sand or any such thing. It can also be a direct connection you have with him."

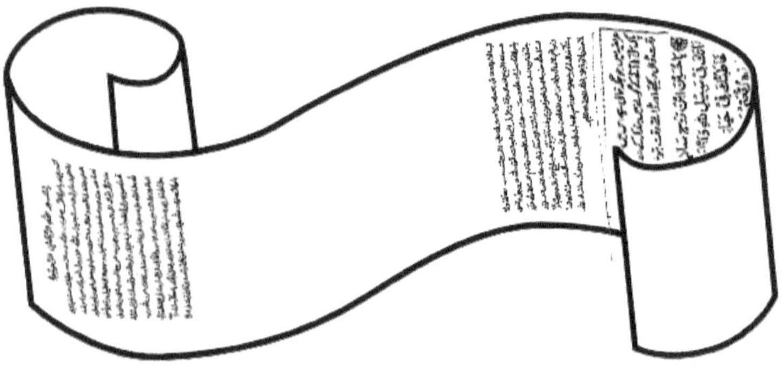

At Imran's surprised look, Mrs. Hudda answered his unasked question. "Yes, sometimes when you are so close with someone you can have a direct link and just talk to him straight. Though we can't see him, he does hear us."

"My mommy always makes me say salaam to Imam Mahdi (AS) every day, because she says it's wajib to reply, so he will always reply to my salaam even if I don't hear him," Sabira gushed.

"That's very true, Sabira, we should all do that. Now everyone go to your desks and write a letter to Imam Madhi (AS)."

"I really wish I could see him! It's not fair, I want to see the Imam of my time" Jawaad complained.

"You know what, Jawad? You just reminded me. Please pass one of these out to everyone."

"I will give one to you too, Asiya!" Jawad exclaimed frustrated, as Asiya tried to peek at the piece of paper Jawad was handing out to everyone. Asiya sat down with an anxious smile and whispered "We're going on a REAL field trip!" to Sabira.

Sensing the anticipation in the students, Mrs. Hudda started to explain: "These are permission slips for a field trip. We are going to a place that is connected to our 12th Imam, Imam Madhi (AS), which will allow us to get a better understanding of him inshAllah," Mrs. Hudda announced.

She smiled at the students as their jaws dropped. No teacher in the past ever dared to think about taking students of Class 786 on a field trip! Did they hear her correctly? Was this really happening? Where were they going? Some place connected to the twelfth Imam?

Yasir tugged at Taha who was sitting beside him, "Do you think Mrs. Hudda will take us to visit Imam Mahdi (AS)? He is alive you know, maybe that's why we can't time travel like we did for the other 13 Masumeen." Taha shrugged his shoulders bewildered. The children sat at their desks thinking about how blessed they were to be able to visit a holy place.

After looking over the permission slips, the students sat at their desks and poured their hearts out into their aridhas, gave them to Mrs. Hudda and rushed home so they could get their parents to fill out the permission forms.

Name: Hassan

Title: al-Askari

Father: Imam Ali an-Naqi

Mother: Hadis Saleel

Children: Imam Mahdi

Birthday: 9th Rabbiul Akhar 232 AH

Born in Medina

Imam for 6 Years

Died on 8th Rabi Awwal 260 AH at the age of 28

Buried in Samarra Iraq

Use this page to jot down anything you learned and that you think you can apply to your life.

Final
Voyage
Imam al-Mahdi
(A.S)

Mrs. Hudda walked into Class 786 the following week and saw Mr. Hashim sitting with the children. They were having a halaqa session. The children were sharing all the knowledge they had gained about the Masumeen in this semester's Islamic History class.

"Mr. Hashim, Mr. Hashim, did you know Imam Ali (AS) was born in the Kaaba, and that he was so close to Allah that he gave Zakat while he was praying?" Aliya said enthusiastically.

"Mr. Hashim it's my turn now, let me tell you all about Imam Muhammed al-Baqir (AS) and his knowledge. He and his son, Imam Jafar as-Sadiq (AS) are the founders of universities and many of the things we study today in school like Science, Math… CAN YOU BELIEVE THAT?!" Jawad exclaimed.

"And, you gotta get a copy of Imam Ridha (AS)'s golden treatise. It tells you what foods you should eat in the different seasons. Even Mamun, the eighth Imam's biggest enemy, was so impressed with it, he had it inscribed in GOLD" said Aunali.

Mrs. Hudda thanked Allah SWT for guiding these children and instilling love in their hearts for the Ahlul Bayt. She slowly tiptoed into the classroom and joined the halaqa. The children were so engrossed in discussing they didn't even know she was there. You could see the difference in the students of Class 786. They were no longer rowdy, mean, or rude. It seemed as if the traits of the Masumeen like humility, piety, and kindness had trickled into their little hearts. They were thirsty for knowledge and eager to apply everything they learnt in their lives.

"Mrs. Hudda! When did you get here?" Sayyada questioned in amazement. Mrs. Hudda's warm smile sent tingles down the kids. They knew she was so proud of them. Mr. Hashim stood up and told the children how impressed he was with their progress. He prayed to the Almighty that He continues to guide them and inshAllah blesses them with the opportunity to be among the companions of Imam Mahdi (AS).

"Ameen!" the entire class said unanimously.

"Have a safe and wonderful trip," said Mr. Hashim as he left the classroom.

Taha pulled Imran aside, "You know Yasir thinks that Mrs. Hudda might be taking us to see Imam Mahdi (AS)." Everyone's eyes fell on Taha and Imran, as they overheard their conversation. Their eyes quickly turned to Mrs. Hudda in anticipation.

Mrs. Hudda told the children to sit at their desks for a moment.

"When we visited the Ahlul Bayt we all saw how much hatred the enemies of Islam had for them and their companions. In Masjid al-Kufa, Imam Ali (AS) was killed while he was in Sajdah. On the plains of Kerbala, Imam Hussain (AS) was heartlessly massacred, and on the bridge of Baghdad lay the abandoned body of Imam Musa al-Kadhim (AS). The enemies of Islam still exist today and they too want to kill the last living Imam. Out of His mercy, Allah SWT has protected Imam Madhi (AS)," she started to explain.

Jawad interrupted Mrs. Hudda, "That was a different time Mrs. Hudda. I can help protect Imam Madhi (AS). I have a lot of muscles. I eat a lot of spinach!"

"Me too, I will help Imam!" "Yes, me also!" "Yup, so will I!" they all chanted in unison. "Labayk Ya Imam!"

They saw a glimpse of sadness in Mrs. Hudda's eyes. "We all have come a long way in reforming ourselves but there is still so much we need to do. The truth is Imam Mahdi (AS) only needs 313 true believers and helpers in order for him to reappear," she continued.

"What, only 313? But there are more than a billion Muslims in this world!" Sibtain wondered aloud, confused.

"Yes, Sibtain, but out of all those people there aren't even 313 true believers that would give up everything and come to the aid of the Imam if he were to return. Look at us, we always called ourselves Muslims but remember how we used to act before we met Mrs. Hudda, who taught us through the Masumeen, how true Muslims should behave. We need to work harder to have all the good characteristics and serve Allah SWT sincerely," Sabira reminded him and everyone else.

"So we can't meet Imam Mahdi?" asked Imran sadly. "So what's the point of having an Imam that we can't meet?"

The whole class was disappointed; some of them really believed they were going to go on a field trip to visit Imam Mahdi (AS). Mrs. Hudda started to explain "There are people who have met the Imam of our time. When people are in such dire need and call him to help, he comes to help them. At that time they may not realize that it was the Imam until afterwards when they reflect over it. This is a mercy from Allah and a way He can protect the identity of the Imam until we are ready for him. The Imam is also there during Hajj every year and also attends the funeral of a Muslim who has completed all his wajib acts. There are many hadith that say that he also visits the land of Kerbala during Arbaeen. We may not be able to meet him today but we should aim to be among his companions when he returns."

Aunali thoughtfully asked

Mrs. Hudda's face lit up and her smile was ear to ear. "That's a brilliant question, and the answer is so simple. Perfect your wajib acts and hold on to the Qur'an and Ahlul Bayt. If you look at the blackboard, there is a list of 12 out of the 26 promises that the "313 companions" will make to the Imam. We should also make a promise to Imam Mahdi (AS) that we will also try not to do the bad things on this list and do the good things on the list. This might get us closer to being among his companions, inshAllah."

*Not to steal

*Not to abuse a Muslim

*Not to violate anyone's honor

*Not to harm anyone

*Not to unjustly take the property of an orphan

*Not give false testimony

*Not to forsake the masjid

*Be content with little

*Stay away from uncleanliness

*Do Amr bil ma'ruf and Nahyi anil munkar (Enjoin Good and Forbid Evil)

*Wear simple clothes

*Strive in Allah's way as this is His right

After the children read the list, Mrs. Hudda explained that Imam Madhi (AS) has said that those who make these promises will stay close to him, and they will be one of his companions when he returns.

Fizza looked puzzled. "He only needs 313 companions to battle ALL the injustice?"

Mrs. Hudda explained "313 believers will be the first ones to respond and will serve as the leaders of the Imam's army. Of the 313, fifty will be women. After 313, there will be thousands who join him. But there will also be thousands who are against him. We have to make sure we are the ones who will not be against him."

Imran was still having a hard time understanding how the Imam would fight all the injustice in the world. "How will the Imam rule over the whole wide world? I am sure some people won't like that and will try to fight him, wouldn't they?" he asked.

"A lot of the people who benefit from the injustice currently will definitely resist the Imam and won't like the way he rules. But don't worry, Allah is going to send someone very special to help him."

"Wow! This just gets more and more exciting!!" Sayyedah interrupted.

"Who is it?" asked Ammar.

Mrs. Hudda's smiled widened. "It is Prophet Isa (AS) or Jesus as he is commonly known. He will descend from the Heavens and play a big role in convincing the genuine Christians and Jews that Imam Mahdi is the rightful leader. This will inshAllah bring all of humanity together under the banner of Justice. It is also narrated that the Imam will lead Prophet Isa and other followers in prayer."

"Wow! Wouldn't it be the most amazing thing to pray behind the Imam?" Aunali said in excitement. Everyone agreed, it would be such an honor to serve the Imam after his reappearance and pray behind him.

RING! RING! RING!

Mrs. Hudda's phone rang. The bus to take the children to the airport was here.

"Let's finish our conversation on Imam Madhi during our trip to Samarra, Iraq, to visit the

Askarian Shrine. This was where the eleventh Imam lived and the place where Imam Mahdi (AS) was born and went into ghaybah after the martyrdom of his father," Mrs. Hudda told the class.

The children all fell down in prostration. As they put their head down, tears trickled down their cheeks. "Alhamdulillah" was echoed throughout the room. They were so thrilled. They were going to visit the tenth and eleventh Imam's graves and the basement from which Imam Mahdi (AS) went into ghayba. They all rushed to get their bags and followed Mrs. Hudda to the bus.

Orlando International Airport

312

"Can you believe this Sumayya? We are actually going to travel to Iraq to the house where Imam Madhi (AS) was born!" Fizza squealed excitedly as they arrived at the Orlando International Airport. They quickly checked in, grabbed their boarding passes and ran to the gate that their flight was going to leave from. This was going to be a trip of a lifetime! The entire class was ecstatic!

"You know, even though we can't see Imam Mahdi, I really think he got my letter, because what I asked for happened!" Hadi whispered to Aunali who whispered it to Talib who shared it with Imran. Soon after, everyone was talking about their aridhas that they wrote to the Imam and felt that they knew that Imam Mahdi (AS) had received their letters even though they couldn't directly communicate with him.

"Excuse me, Ladies and Gentlemen, we are sorry but there will be a slight delay due to the weather conditions in New York. We thank you in advance for your patience," a staff member of Hud Hud Airlines Flight 786110 announced.

The smiles on the children's faces turned upside down into frowns. As time went by, they started getting more and more disappointed and their eyes kept steering to the gate window to where their plane was just sitting. Mrs. Hudda tried to calm them down, reminding them of what they had learnt from the Masumeen about being patient. The children tried their hardest but they began to cry as their hopes of visiting Samarra were slowly being shattered.

"Man this stinks, what if the weather doesn't get better in New York? Do you know the other airlines have already canceled 100 flights?" Shabbir worried.

Mrs. Hudda gathered all the children around her. "While we're waiting to board the plane, how about we sit in a little circle and try to learn a little bit about the Imam of our time, Imam Mahdi (AS). Everything happens for a reason. Maybe Allah SWT wants us to know more about the Imam of our time. We won't be able to be his companions until we really know and love him! So, who will start us off? Who were the parents of Imam Mahdi (A.S.)?"

"That's an easy one, Mrs. Hudda, we just saw him on our last trip. The eleventh Imam, Imam

Hassan Askari was his father!" Asiya confidently answered.

"And we also saw his mom. Her name was Lady Narjis Khatoon!" Aliya added.

"That's awesome! Let's see, does anyone know anything more about his mom?" Mrs. Hudda continued to question.

Yasir scratched his head while Taha looked at Ammar for an answer. Looking at the blank look on all the children's faces, Mrs. Hudda continued. "Lady Narjis Khatoon was a Roman princess. She came to Baghdad from Rome. It's a really special story of how she got married to Imam Hassan Askari (AS). Allah SWT had chosen Lady Nargis Khatoon to be the one who gives birth to the last Imam. Through dreams and the help of the tenth Imam, she was guided to Imam Hassan Askari (AS) and they got married. You have to remember that the tenth and eleventh Imams spent most of their lives in prison or under house arrest so the wedding and the birth of the twelfth Imam were a secret."

Amina interrupted, "That's right, I remember when we went to see Imam Hassan Askari (AS) the people had already heard of the prophecy of the last Imam who would come into this world and fill it with justice. The Imams that had come before him always talked about it. The enemies of the Ahlul Bayt wanted to stop him from being born. That was the reason they imprisoned Imam Hassan Askari (AS) for most of his life."

"But Mrs. Hudda, umm... I don't want to be silly or anything, but can't you tell when a woman is pregnant? I remember my mom looked like she had a watermelon in her tummy before my brother was born!" Sayyida said.

"HAHAHAHAHA!" everyone started to giggle and laugh. Mrs. Hudda also had a grin on her face. "Yes…most women do become bigger but this pregnancy was special because Lady Narjis

Khatoon was going to give birth to an Imam and Allah SWT protects his Imams. The pregnancy was a secret and no one could tell that she was even pregnant. This shows that if Allah SWT wills for something to happen, it WILL happen, and HE will always take care of HIS creations."

"Mrs. Hudda," Imran interrupted, "I still don't get it. How can Imam Mahdi (AS) be there if we can't see him, if he can't talk to us! How can he help us if he isn't physically here?"

Before Mrs. Hudda could respond, there was an announcement. "Ladies and gentlemen, boys and girls, your prayers have been answered. The sun's rays behind the clouds has warmed up the air and the bad weather has  cleared. Please prepare to board the aircraft in the next few minutes."

"Whohooohooo, Alhamdulillah!" the children all cheered.

Mrs. Hudda smiled. "SubhanAllah! What a great example to help me answer Imran's questions. Allah SWT truly guides those who He wants to."

The entire class was intrigued and decided to listen in. "Imran, have you ever noticed how even on a cloudy day, we can still feel the warmth of the sun and can still benefit from it? Even when the sun is covered by the clouds and cannot be seen, we know it is still there because its rays still surround the Earth and the entire creation of Allah SWT benefits from it. Similarly, the Imam of the time himself has said,

'As for deriving benefit from me in my ghayba; it is like deriving benefit from the sun when it is behind the clouds.'

Just like on a cloudy day, we eagerly wait for the sun to come out, our minds race with thoughts of what we will do on that nice sunny day, or how refreshing ice cream will be as it melts in our mouths. In the same manner, we should also be eagerly awaiting our Imam and never lose hope in his reappearance. I want you to ponder over this, during the long summer days, when the heat can be so excruciating, as sweat drips from our foreheads, we realize the value of the clouds that bring with them cool air. Similarly, with our Imam, he is hidden from us so we realize the importance of who he really is and the message of Allah SWT. We also realize that we need to prepare ourselves for him. So our minds should have thoughts of what WE need to fix in ourselves so we can benefit from him."

The entire class started to smile. Their hearts were content as the words of the Imam spoke to the core of their hearts. They knew that the Imam of our time - Imam Mahdi (AS) was with them, just like the sun behind the clouds, and now they needed to focus on how to prepare for his arrival.

"This is the final boarding call for Hud Hud Flight 786110 to New York. All passengers please board at gate 12."

"See, if you have patience and faith, if it is meant for us to go to Samarra, then we will inshAllah! Grab your stuff and let's get on board!" Mrs. Hudda reminded them as they celebrated.

Hud Hud Airlines Flight 786110 made a safe and smooth landing in New York.

"Gather around everyone, this is our first stopover. We have about 2 hours before our next flight takes off for Baghdad. Let's find a place to sit and enjoy our homemade chicken sandwiches," Mrs. Hudda said as she passed out the yummy sandwiches.

Boy, were they hungry! As they were gobbling down the food, Taha asked Mrs. Hudda something that had been bugging him. "If everything surrounding the eleventh Imam's marriage and the birth of Imam Mahdi was a secret, then how did the people find out about Imam Mahdi (AS) in the first place?"

Mrs. Hudda wiped her mouth, said "Alhamdulillah" and began to explain. "After Imam Hassan Askari (AS) was martyred and Salaat al-Mayyit was being recited, the eleventh Imam's brother, Jaffer, started to lead the prayers.

All of a sudden a 5 year old boy went up to Jaffer and said 'I will lead the prayer as he is my father.' Everyone in the crowd was astonished! That's how they found out that the twelfth Imam had already been born, the Imam that will bring justice to the world."

"Soon after that, the evil men of the Caliph Mutamid went looking for Imam Mahdi (AS) so they could kill him. They searched his house but couldn't find anyone. When they went to the basement it seemed as if it was filled with water, and floating on top was a prayer mat with a 5 year old boy praying."

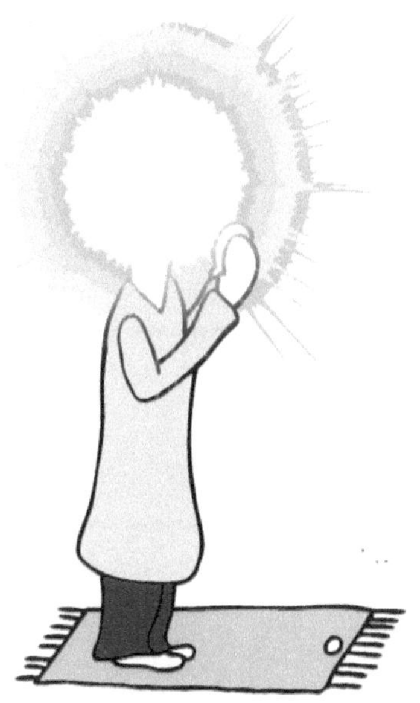

"As they tried to get to him, Allah SWT protected the Imam and it was as if Imam Mahdi (AS) vanished! That was the beginning of his first period called Ghaybat al-Sughra - The Minor Occultation - where he is concealed from us. Imam Mahdi spent a total of 70 years in Ghaybat al-Sughra. In this time he didn't leave the Muslims without guidance; he had 4 loyal people who acted like messengers between him and his Shia. After the Ghaybat al-Sughra ended, he went into Ghaybat al-Kubrah – The Major Occultation – and he is in this ghayba till today. That occultation will end when he reappears again."

"This is the final boarding call for Flight 110 non-stop to Baghdad, Iraq. The flight is now boarding at gate 14."

Shabbir smiled, "Gate 14, that's a lucky number because Imam Madhi (AS) is the 14th Masumeen!"

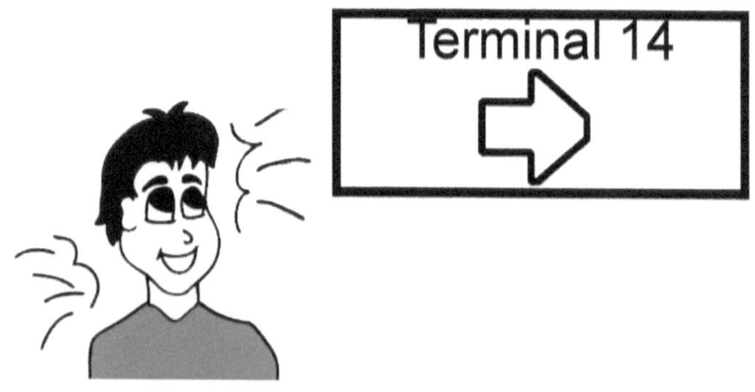

The flight to Iraq was very long. The kids were getting anxious, they just couldn't wait. Aunali and Imran were reflecting on how the Imam is just like the sun behind a cloud. "Do you think that Imam Mahdi can help you in an emergency?" Imran asked Aunali.

"Imam Mahdi! I know him, he helped me," said a young girl who was sitting in front of them.

The little girl stopped playing with her toys and started jumping up and down. "I know him, Mummy."

Imran looked at Aunali and then looked at the lady sitting next to the little girl. "How? Where? When? Is she for real or is she just joking? What is she talking about?"

The little girl's mom saw the curiosity in their eyes and began to explain. "We had gone for Hajj a while back, there were so many believers from all around the world that also came for Hajj. Our daughter got separated from us and was lost in the crowd. All of us were very worried for her and looked everywhere but we could not see her in the sea of people..."

"She was scared as well. After all, she was in the

middle of strangers and could not find her family. She remembered her aunt telling her if she ever needed help to call on the Imam. So she prayed to Allah SWT and to Imam Mahdi (AS) to come to help her."

"In no time, a pious gentleman came towards her and asked her if she was alright. He helped her finish her tawaf and then he helped her find our group. We all realised that the Imam hears us when we call him sincerly, and he sends help to us in different ways."

Imran and Aunali had goose bumps and were overcome with amazement. Imran thoughtfully asked "Do you think we could be supporters of the Imam?"

The lady replied, "Most definitely! Whenever you see someone in need, help them in any way you can in the name of the Imam and stop doing things the Imam doesn't like, and you will be counted among his supporters InshAllah, just like the kind man who helped my daughter!"

Aunali and Imran looked at each other in awe. They were starting to see that even though Imam Mahdi (AS) is hidden from us, he truly is there and is always watching over us. They realised that they don't have to wait for the Imam to return before they can be one his helpers, they can be a helper of the Imam right now by looking after those in need! Before they could thank the lady, they were interrupted by an announcement from the pilot. "Flight attendants, please prepare for landing."

"We are here, we are here! Pinch me, I can't believe it!" shouted Sabira as the kids came out of the Airport and into the terminal at Baghdad International Airport. Their eyes widened as they saw the Muslim culture everywhere.

"It feels great to be in a Muslim country!" Sabira excitedly told everyone.

An old, humble looking man and a younger man who looked like a slightly older version of Mrs. Hudda, came towards them. Mrs. Hudda hugged both men and turned to the children.

"This is my father, Haider and that's Mustafa, my brother. My brother volunteered to help us out on this trip. My father and Mustafa will take us on a drive to the Askarian shrine. The children greeted the two men.

Together they walked out of the airport. They got into the back of a huge white bus while Mustafa and Haider sat in the front. As they drove further into the countryside, they looked through the bus windows and observed how people lived in Iraq. They saw some rich neighborhoods and some very poor ones as well. They all started to smile when they saw little kids their age playing on the roads. The kids on the street stopped to look and wave at the bus full of kids! The bus stopped after a couple of hours of driving, at a tiny house in the middle of the rural area between Baghdad and Samarra. Mustafa and Haider got out of the bus.

"Is this it?"

"Is this where Imam Hassan al-Askari is buried?"

"Do you think maybe, just maybe, Imam Mahdi (AS) will still be in the basement?"

Questions and questions and questions could be heard throughout the bus. Were they just moments away from seeing the place where Imam Mahdi (AS) went into ghaybah? Were their feet going to be stepping on the same spots the Ahlul Bayt stepped on?

"Look, there is Mustafa Uncle," Sabira pointed. Mustafa approached Mrs. Hudda with a sad look on his face. "My dear sister, I think we have a flat tire. We will have to stop here and fix it. It might take a while." As Mustafa and Haider were fixing the tire, Mrs. Hudda used this time to discuss Imam Mahdi further. She looked at Sibtain and asked, "Why the long face, the tire will be fixed in no time, we will be on our way to Samarra soon inshAllah."

"I don't like waiting!" Sibtain snapped.

Mrs. Hudda smiled gently and put her arm around Sibtain. "I know, waiting and being patient is hard, and although we might want things to happen quickly, sometimes it is better if we wait, we can use our time to learn something and improve ourselves. So, when we are waiting for the Imam to return, we should be patient and try to improve ourselves so we are ready for the Imam when he arrives inshAllah."

Sibtain was still upset. "But… I am sad that he is hidden from us. It's just not fair."

Mrs. Hudda told the kids to look inside their pockets and take out their sunglasses. She asked them to first look out the window. Then she told them to look out the window again but this time wearing their sunglasses. The children peered out the window and saw the same exact things but in a darker shade. Just then another bus pulled over next to their bus and the children could no longer see out the window. She told the children that is also how Imam Mahdi (AS) is like the sun behind the clouds. When the cloud is covering the sun, the rays still touch the Earth, but the Earth absorbs the rays in different levels. Sometimes, the trees will block the ground from absorbing the rays, sometimes the tall buildings will block the rays… Imam Mahdi may be hidden from us, but his guidance is always there. It is our souls who are not absorbing his guidance. We have to examine ourselves and see what we are doing wrong in our life, that we cannot connect to Imam Mahdi (AS) and absorb his guidance and knowledge.

The children all looked at one another. They finally realized that they weren't ready for the Imam. They needed to change their lifestyles, spend less time watching rubbish on the television, be kinder to their parents, perfect their wajibaat, read and UNDERSTAND the Qur'an, stop listening to music and do whatever they could to stop injustice. The children realized it was some of their actions that didn't allow them to see the Imam.

As they sat and reflected, Mustafa and Haider came in and gave them good news. The tire was fixed and they were less than a hundred miles from Samarra. The children were very happy and energized by the good news.

"Mrs. Hudda, how will we know when Imam Mahdi (AS) will reappear?" Fizza questioned.

"Oh Fizza, only Allah SWT knows when Imam Madhi (AS) will come back to us. However, narrations from the Masumeen tell us of some signs of his reappearance. These are things that will happen before Imam Mahdi reappears."

Mrs. Hudda then started reading some of the signs from a book she was holding:

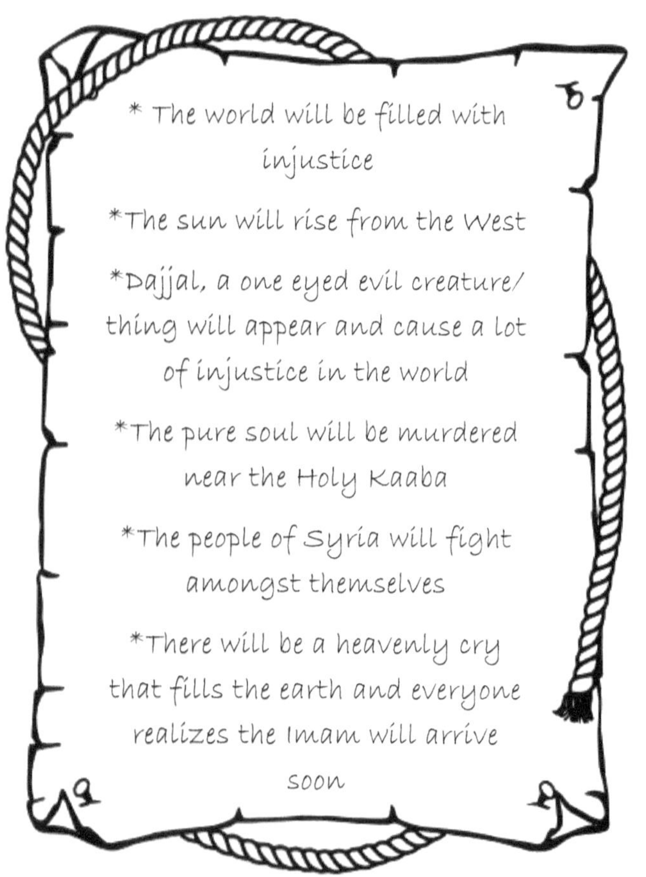

Before Mrs. Hudda could finish the list, Mustafa interrupted her. They were here.

The children's eyes welled up at the sight of the Askarian Shrine. Tears trickled down and flushed their cheeks. The remnants of the bomb explosion could still be seen.

Sabira was so upset. "This is the place where the Imam of the time's father and grandfather are buried. It's in ruins. You can see the damage the bombing has done."

The entire class was heartbroken. They slowly walked inside and paid their respects to the two Imams buried there. They then sat outside in the courtyard.

"I say it's halaqa time," Shabbir exclaimed. All the kids nodded in agreement. They felt so honored that they were sitting on such a holy land, discussing about the holiest people to have ever lived.

Aunali started off, "I think it's so important that we create a bond between us and the Imam of our time. I did some research and there are several ways we can stay close to our Imam. We can go to visit the shrines of the other Masumeen and seek closeness to him through them. I heard he visits the land of Kerbala on 15th Shabaan and Arbaeen."

Summayya wanted to add her two cents as well. "We can read more about him. We need to find good books. The more we know about him, the stronger our bond can be."

"We can also write aridhas, talk to him from our heart, I know he listens" shared Sibtain.

Mrs. Hudda thought this was the perfect time to teach the children about Du'a Ahad. "There is one prayer you can recite to help strengthen your bond with Imam Madhi (AS). It is called Du'a Ahad. It is said if you recite it for 40 mornings, you may be counted amongst the helpers of Imam Mahdi.

If you die before the Imam reappears, Allah SWT will raise you from the dead so you can help the Imam of the time, inshAllah."

Mrs. Hudda passed around a copy of the du'a and the class recited it together with the translation to help them connect with the Imam.

As they recited the du'a, tears started flowing down their cheeks, full of hope that Allah SWT fulfills their du'a, especially when they recited:

"O Allah renew for him my promise, pledge and allegiance on my neck in the morning of this day of mine and whatever days (of my life) I live. I shall never turn away from it nor let it ever vanish."

O Allah make me one of his helpers, aides, and his protectors. Those who hurry to fulfill his commands and obey his orders. Those who are his supporters and compete with each other to (fulfill) his intention and seek martyrdom in his presence.

After reading the du'a, the children's hearts were at peace. Mrs. Hudda led the children to the basement from where Imam Madhi went into ghaybah.

"I can't believe this is the place where Imam disappeared from," said Sumayya.

"I can't believe we are standing in the same place where Imam Mahdi was, I wish I could be his companion," exclaimed Fizza.

Mrs. Hudda wiped the tears from her eyes and shared a hadith from the Imams. "Imam Zain al-Abideen and Imam Baqir (AS) have said, 'When the Qaim (Imam Mahdi) reappears, each one of our followers will be more daring than a lion. Allah will make their hearts like pieces of iron and he will make the strength of one man equal to the strength of 40 men'."

As the children all shared their feelings, they could feel an inner strength as well as strength coming from another source, a higher power. Their minds were racing with thoughts of how they needed to commit themselves to Allah, the Ahlul Bayt, their community and society. How they needed to follow in the footsteps of the fourteen Masumeen. Not just talk the talk but walk the walk! How they need to work hard to stop the oppression that is happening in the world.

Imran started to cry out, "Just looking at the holy shrine, reminds me of all the oppression that is happening in the world today. It hurts so much seeing how much injustice is occurring. Not only were these Imams oppressed during their lifetime, but they continue to be oppressed after martyrdom as well! Where are you O Awaited One? Where are you? We need you!"

The class start chanting, and their eyes poured like a waterfall.

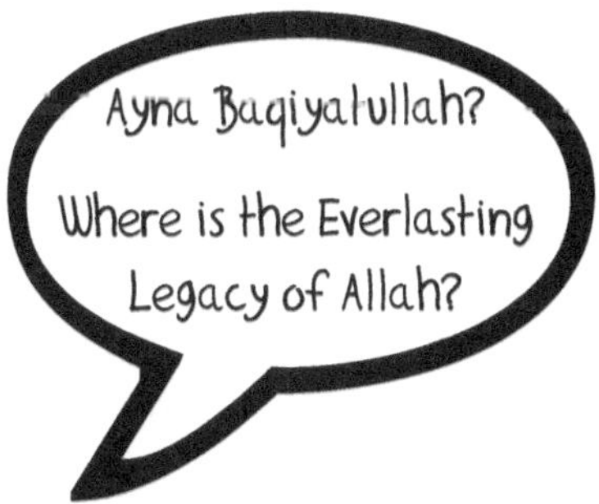

Before they could take another step, they realized their pockets were glowing. Each child put their hand in their pocket and pulled out that tiny shiny clay piece with words engraved on it that they had received from their journeys visiting the other Masumeen.

Yasir and Sibtain bumped into each other accidently and their pieces fell to the ground and clung to each other like a jigsaw puzzle.

"Look, they are connected! They all belong with each other as if they are pieces to a puzzle. Come on everyone, put your pieces together!" Yasir said anxiously.

Ammaar connected his *Du'a* piece with Sibtain's *Faith* piece, who connected it to Fizza's *Generosity* piece that connected to Yasir's piece that had *Salaat* engraved on it. Jawad connected his piece that said *Peace and Anger Management* to Taha's piece that said *Sacrifice*. Sayyada connected her *Truthful* with Shabbir's *Knowledge*, who connected it to Asiya's *Humility* that was then connected to Sumayya's *Intelligence* and Sabira's *Kindness*. Aliya connected her *Patience* to Amina's *Multi-Talented* which was then connected to Hadi's *Selflessness*.

"I guess I have the last piece, *Always stay close to the Imams*," Imran said as he connected his piece to the puzzle. When all the pieces were connected they formed a seal. It looked beautiful and was glowing; all the childrens' hands were on it.

They looked at Mrs. Hudda who was nodding her head up and down. "Each one of you had a piece of the seal. Our Masumeen are our road map to please the Almighty. If we learn and practice all the virtues they have taught us, we will be with the

Imam of our time, Imam Mahdi (AS). We have to have hearts stronger than lions and the will to stop the injustice.

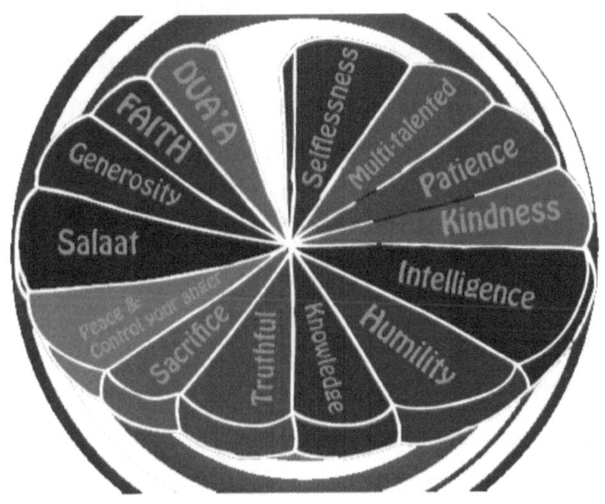

As they looked at the seal one more time, they gathered to recite Dua Ahad in the same place Imam Mahdi (AS) went into ghayba from. With smiles in their hearts, they put their hands together and said

It was getting late, Mrs. Hudda instructed the kids to start heading back to the bus. As they headed back, the clouds above separated and the sun began to glow with a brilliant shine. The children smiled, remembering the Imam is always with them. The air around them became warm and they felt tingles through their little bodies.

Suddenly a heavenly cry penetrated the earth in all directions.

What was that? They all wondered, wide-eyed and staring at each other and Mrs. Hudda in astonishment. Was this the heavenly cry that Mrs. Hudda was telling them about? Could this be the sign that the Imam was going to reappear soon?

Thump! Thump! Thump! The hearts of the students of Class 786 started racing. How much time do they have to prepare themselves to be the companions of Imam Mahdi (AS)? They are now racing against the clock. Will they make it?

LOOK AT WHAT IS GOING ON IN THE WORLD TODAY

HOW MUCH TIME DO YOU HAVE TO PREPARE FOR HIS ARRIVAL?

LABAYK YA
iMAM!

Also Published by Sun Behind The Cloud...

Get your copy by visiting

www.sunbehindthecloud.com